SPEAKING

TEACHER'S BOOK

ENGLISH FOR ACADEMIC STUDY SERIES

SPEAKING

Teacher's Book

Clare Furneaux and Mark Rignall

PRENTICE HALL
EUROPE

The authors would like to thank Anne Pallant for her help with earlier drafts of this book.

The authors and publishers would also like to thank the following for permission to reproduce copyright material in this book:

BBC English for extracts from *Britain Now* © Catherine Addis (1992), published by the British Broadcasting Corporation, in The Family in Britain Text B; Channel Four Television for extracts from *Faces of the Family* by Tobe Aleksander (1994) in The Family in Britain Text A.

First published in 1997 by
Prentice Hall Europe
Campus 400, Spring Way
Maylands Avenue, Hemel Hempstead
Hertfordshire, HP2 7EZ
© International Book Distributors Ltd 1997

Printed and bound in Great Britain by Redwood Books, Trowbridge, Wiltshire

British Library Cataloguing in Publication Data

A catalogue record for this book is available from the British Library

ISBN 0-13-507583-1

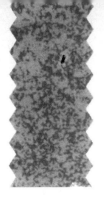

CONTENTS

MAP OF THE COURSE

UNIT	TOPIC	SKILLS FOCUS	LANGUAGE HELP
Foundation	You and your course	Exchanging information	Repair expressions
1	Countries	Preparing a presentation	Asking questions after a presentation
2	The home	Preparing for your audience	Describing an object
3	Education	Looking for ideas to shape your talk	Signpost expressions
4	The family	Collecting information	Comparison and contrast Describing trends
5	The media	Giving an overview	Asking for clarification
6	Health	Preparing a group presentation	Expressing proportion
7	Population and migration	Responding to questions	Describing trends Cause and effect Responding to questions
8	Defence	Generating ideas	Expressing opinion Agreeing and disagreeing
9	Parapsychology	Rehearsing and evaluation	Referring to a text Expressing opinion
10	Studying in a new environment	Summarising in discussion	Deduction

SOURCE MATERIAL/TAPESCRIPT[1]	LEARNER DIARY THEME
Chart 1: Male and Female student numbers (p71) Chart 2: Home and international student numbers (p74) Listening text 1: John Mitchell (p83) Listening text 2: Catherine Andrews (p85)	Previous experience
(Information from self/class)	Making a presentation
Listening text: The Home in Britain (p88)	Expanding your vocabulary
Listening text: The English Education System (p89)	Pronunciation
Reading Text A: The Family in Britain (p68) Reading Text B: The Family in Britain (p72)	Taking part in a discussion
Chart 1 Programme-hours by category(p67) Chart 2 Production-cost by category (p75) Chart 3 Production-cost by hour (p79) Listening text 1: Peter Capes (p91) Listening text 2: Peter Capes (p93)	Taking stock
(Information from class)	Team-work
Chart 1 World population growth (p66) Chart 2 Legal immigrants admitted to the US (p63) Reading text A: Mass migration in modern era (p70) Reading text B: Mass migration in modern era (p98)	Talking about a written text
Listening extract A: Captain Johnson (p97) Listening extract A: Captain Johnson (p98)	Talking about a spoken text
Reading text A: Putting telepathy to the test (p64) Reading text B: Putting telepathy to the text (p76) Reading text C: Putting telepathy to the test (p80)	Presenting a point of view
Listening text 1 International student (p100) Listening text 2 British student (p103)	

1. Page numbers in this column refer to the Student's Book.

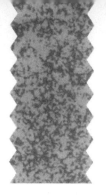

INTRODUCTION

AIMS OF THE COURSE

This course is designed for students who are planning to study at a college or university where the language of instruction is English. It aims to help them to develop the oral communication skills in English that are needed for academic study. In particular, it aims to improve their ability to:

- give short oral presentations effectively
- contribute to seminar discussions appropriately and fluently
- follow the contributions made to the discussion by others
- assess their performance in discussion and presentation tasks.

The primary focus of the course is on skill development rather than on the presentation of new language at one specific level. It is suitable for intermediate and upper-intermediate learners of English; we recommend a minimum starting level of IELTS[1] band 5, or TOEFL[2] 490. It can be used successfully both by those who have little experience of study skills, and also by those who have good study skills in their own language and now need to practise using them in English.

CONTENTS

The course consists of a Foundation Unit followed by ten standard units. Each unit of material requires three to four hours of work in the classroom and 30 to 60 minutes of preparation by the learner.

Each unit guides the learner through a sequence of activities: he[3] identifies issues related to the unit topic, extracts relevant information from the texts provided or from other sources, then puts his ideas forward in discussion and/or presentation. This sequence reflects the basic study cycle (see Figure 1, page x), which students have to follow on virtually all academic courses. The unit thus provides a context for authentic practice of precisely those oral communication skills that are needed for academic study at an English-medium college or university.

In each unit there is a focus on a particular aspect of discussion or presentation (e.g. giving an overview, or responding to questions after a presentation). The units also guide the learner to make use of the learning aids at the back of the book: the Independent Learner section on pages 106-122 of the Student's Book, and the Language Help section on pages 123-141 of the Student's Book, which

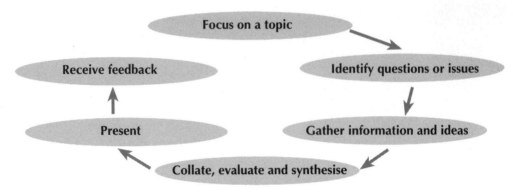

Figure 1: The basic study cycle

presents key language organised according to function (such as **Describing trends**, or **Expressing proportion**). These aids are designed to be of use both during and after the course.

The unit topics are intended to be accessible and stimulating, but suitable at the same time for the relatively formal, academic type of treatment that EAP[4] learners need to practise. The tasks do not require any specialist, subject-specific knowledge beyond what can be extracted from the Source Material section at the back of the Student's Book. Learners can therefore concentrate on skill development without the distraction of having to master a whole new body of knowledge, and classes can be mixed as far as the students' subject specialisms are concerned.

PRINCIPLES FOR TEACHERS

The following principles shaped the design of this course and should guide the practice of teachers using it.

Focus on skill

To study in a foreign language, it is not enough simply to have an advanced knowledge of the language; it is necessary to be able to use that knowledge skilfully to carry out a range of study tasks. Two of the oral communication skills that are called on repeatedly at various stages of the study cycle are those of discussion and presentation.[5] Discussion and presentation in a foreign language are complex skills, and the EAP learner therefore needs both to practise each of them as a whole, and to analyse and assess his performance of specific aspects of them.

Language resource improvement

As well as practising the skilled use of their existing language resources in English, EAP learners need to improve and expand those resources. Each unit in this course therefore refers the learner to relevant pages in the Language Help section, which presents lexis and structures in fourteen key functional areas. At the end of each unit is a language review task, which asks the learner to extend or create a map of vocabulary related to the unit topic, and to reread and extend specific pages of the Language Help section.

Practical advice for teachers:

- Monitor to ensure that each learner finds and implements an effective way of recording and organising his expanding vocabulary.
- Encourage learners to expand the Language Help section by listening and looking out for expressions to add to it.
- Encourage learners to make good use of a monolingual dictionary (e.g. *Oxford Advanced Learners' Dictionary*) and a reference grammar with key (e.g. Raymond Murphy (1994) *English Grammar in Use*, 2nd edn, CUP). Even basic self-access resources such as these are a valuable aid to teacher and learner; they allow the teacher to feed back and guide remediation more efficiently, and enable more independent learning.

The 'fluent but fossilised'[6] learner is common in many EAP classes, particularly amongst students whose formal instruction in English took place some years before. There is a risk that communication practice, if badly managed, will simply reinforce the errors in the English of these learners. The teacher has to take steps to counteract fossilisation by:

- encouraging and helping learners to plan language for a task in advance;
- giving clear feedback on the errors that most affect their performance;
- improvising remedial 'mini-lessons' on specific language items as the need arises in class;
- directing learners towards appropriate remedial work outside the classroom.

Independent learning

Learning is most effective when the learner is actively involved in managing the process. The course aims to enable the learner to take this active role.

The Foundation Unit helps the learner to analyse his needs by informing him of the types of oral communication task that are an integral part of most academic courses at English-speaking colleges and universities. He examines some common attitudes towards learning to speak English, and considers how appropriate they are to his own case. In the Learner Questionnaire, he identifies his 'lacks'[7] (i.e. the progress he needs to make in order to reach the target) and sets his own learning goals.

The Learner Diary at the end of each unit encourages the learner to reflect on his learning, to assess the progress he has made and to plan further improvement. Other activities throughout the course give practice in working collaboratively and in exchanging peer feedback, both of which are likely to be helpful on subsequent courses of study.

Practical advice for teachers:

- Go through the aims and rationale of the course with the learner at the beginning, to help him to relate them to his own aims.

- Encourage the learner to think about the purpose of particular tasks and how he personally can benefit most effectively from them.

- Encourage the learner to use and expand the Language Help section, and to exploit any other self-access resources that are available to him (these might range from a classroom copy of a good English–English dictionary, to video-recordings of seminars).

- Arrange for each learner to give an extended presentation, in the second half of the course, on a topic related to his own academic subject. The presentation could be given either to his normal, mixed class, in which case you would need to remind him of the need to tailor it for a non-specialist audience, or to a group of students whose academic subjects are similar, whom you bring together for the occasion. The Independent Learner section (particularly the checklists and the prompt questions on page 115 of the Student's Book) is designed to support this kind of extension activity.

Maximum feedback

Feedback is essential to learning, and the quality of feedback affects the quality of learning. This course is designed to provide the learner with regular feedback on his performance of discussion and presentation tasks in English. It also helps him develop the skills of giving and seeking effective peer feedback and of self-assessment. A series of checklists (pages 112–113 and 118 of the Student's Book) and a guide to giving feedback effectively (Student's Book page 122) are provided as a common basis for assessment and feedback by the teacher, by peers and by the learner himself.

Giving feedback is one of the teacher's most important functions. On skill-related matters, feedback from the teacher can very usefully be supplemented by peer feedback; on questions specifically related to language, however, the learner will rightly look to the teacher for authoritative feedback.

Practical advice for teachers:

- Soon after the beginning of the course, give each learner a clear, conservative assessment of the current level of his oral interaction skills in English, and of the areas in which he needs to make particular progress. The assessment can be based on his performance in class during the Foundation Unit, or in a special entry or placement test. It can be given in terms of a rating scale such as the IELTS 10-band scale.

- Ensure that the learner does not go through the course with a grossly inaccurate view of the level he has reached. During an intensive course of ten weeks, for example, we recommend that teachers should give the learner a clear report on his progress on at least two occasions, probably in Weeks 5 and 10.

- Make use of the various ways in which feedback can be given: in an immediate intervention or a subsequent review session; to an individual learner or to a group; orally or in writing. A regular tutorial session also provides a convenient opportunity for feedback to the learner.

- For written feedback, use a standard format with which the learner becomes familiar: for example, a pre-printed checklist which the teacher completes (see page 112 of the Student's Book), or a simple feedback note (see page xix of the Teacher's Book).

- Identify in feedback notes the error or point to improve and, whenever possible, suggest remedial action (e.g. to work through the relevant section of a reference grammar with exercises and key; to practise a suitable pronunciation drill in the language laboratory; to listen to specified recorded conversations to discover how native speakers of English achieve a particular communicative goal).

- Set a target for the number of individualised feedback notes you intend to give each learner during the course, and then monitor your progress towards the target. A reasonable target would be five to each learner during a ten week course.

See the section on **Using feedback notes** on pages xix–xx.

Before giving feedback on a presentation, give the speaker the opportunity to voice his own feelings about his performance ('How well do you think it went?' or 'How did you feel about it yourself?'). Similarly, if you ask the class to prepare peer feedback on a presentation made by one of the students, give him the opportunity to air his own view of his performance before he receives their comments. This promotes self-monitoring, and allows the presenter to be the first to point out and perhaps explain any particular difficulties or mishaps that occurred.

TIMETABLING AND SELECTING UNITS

Each unit is divided into three sessions. Sessions 1 and 2 each require 50 to 60 minutes of classroom time; Session 3 requires 80 to 100 minutes[8]. The eleven units of the course therefore require some 35 to 40 hours' work in the classroom.

If you do not have this amount of classroom time available, there are a number of factors to take into consideration in selecting a smaller number of units for use with your class. The Foundation Unit is probably the best place to start, however limited the time available, as it contains useful introductory material. After that, you may want to select the units whose topics you think will be of most interest to your students, or whose skills focus will be of most help to them. If you feel that your students need more practice at listening than reading, or vice versa, or to ensure a balance between the two, you can select units accordingly. The Map of the Course on pages vi–vii is designed to make this kind of selection easier: the column headed **Source material/tapescript** indicates for each unit whether the main source is a listening or a reading text.

STANDARD TASK TYPES

Preparation (e.g. Unit 7, Task 1.5)

EAP learners benefit from taking time to think through the topic and task ahead, and then planning what they want to say and how they can use their language resources in English to say it. This planning stage, requiring learners to think in a focused way about both the *what* (i.e. purpose and content) and the *how* (i.e. language), is an important part of the process by which they can improve their language resources. Encourage them to consult the Language Help section, other language reference works (e.g. dictionary, grammar book), their own records, and you the teacher, as part of this preparation.

The form the planning should take depends on the task ahead: for a short discussion, it may be limited to earmarking selected pages of the Language Help section and jotting down some relevant ideas they want to contribute to the discussion; for a formal presentation, at the other extreme, it will probably involve producing an outline, prompt cards and visual aids.

Language focus (e.g. Unit 9, Task 2.1)

This task focuses the learners' attention on a particular functional area of language which is relevant to the communication task that follows. It asks them to read through one of the Language Help pages and practise producing the expressions given there. It may instruct them to choose two or three expressions to use appropriately in context in the next task. In some cases (e.g. **Describing trends**, a functional area which students had found especially difficult during the trialling of the original version of these materials), the Language Help page includes exercises for more thorough, controlled practice of language form.

The teacher has an important role here. Go through the Language Help page with your class, and for each expression that you think your students will find helpful:

• Model the pronunciation, and drill as appropriate for your students.
• Elicit/establish how it is used, including an example of it in context.

Exchanging information (e.g. Unit 7, Task 1.6)

Make sure that your students take the opportunity offered by information-gap activities to practise their *oral* communication skills in English. You need to check that they do not reveal the information to their partner in its written form (i.e. chart, text, notes) at this stage, or conduct the exchange in a language other than English.

Jigsaw listening (e.g. Foundation Unit, Session 3)

This type of task creates a fairly authentic incentive for listening, note taking and oral summarising. The basic logistical requirement is that half of your students have to listen to Text 1 while the other half listen separately to Text 2. Exactly how you choose to meet this logistical challenge will depend on the classroom space and equipment available in your particular institution. The teachers we have worked with favour a procedure in which pairs of teachers co-ordinate their classes, as follows:

1) Prepare your class for the listening task. Then send half of your students to your colleague's classroom; she sends half of her students to your classroom.

2) All of the students now in your room listen to Text 1 and take notes of the main points. They then compare their notes, and discuss any queries or disagreements that arise, aiming to arrive at a common understanding of the main points. They rewind and replay as necessary for this purpose. (If feasible, allow them to control the cassette player.) In the meantime, all of the students in your colleague's room do likewise with Text 2.

3) All students return to their original classroom. Put your students in pairs (or small groups), matching each 'Text 1 student' with a 'Text 2 student'. Instruct them to exchange information orally.

We have found that the effort required from the teacher to set up a jigsaw listening task is justified by the quality of the practice it affords the student. However, if the conditions in which you teach make this type of task impossible, you could instead conduct a normal, plenary listening task using just one of the two texts.

Review (e.g. Foundation Unit, Task 2.4 and 2.5)

We have included a review stage after certain of the more complex tasks, to ensure that the learner thinks back over his experience of carrying the task out and focuses on what he can learn from it. Unless he deliberately reviews the task in this way, there is a risk that he will not retain the improvement in skill or understanding that he began to make during the task.

Language review (At the end of each Session 3)

The tasks and source material in this course are designed to be authentically academic, so that each unit exposes the learner to a range of language likely to be of use to him in his academic studies. However, because his attention during the unit is often focused on skill or subject matter rather than language, there is a risk that he will not store new language effectively, and consequently will not be able to recall it clearly later on. The Language review task at the end of each unit aims to prevent this from happening, by asking students to review and record useful language according to function and topic.

The Language review asks learners to produce a vocabulary map. In our experience, many EAP learners find this to be a useful technique for vocabulary learning – a good map is generative and memorable. We encourage students to try it as one possible method of organising their vocabulary, but we recognise that it will not suit everyone. The teacher has an important role here in monitoring and guiding learners to ensure that each individual finds a method that is effective for him.

Learner Diary (At the end of each unit)

The concept of a Learner Diary will be new to some learners. When you first introduce this task to your students, refer them to **Keeping a Learner Diary** on pages 110-111 of the Student's Book, which outlines the rationale of the task and gives examples of diary entries. You may want to supplement these with an example of a diary entry of your own, on a poster or OHT, particularly if you are yourself in the process of learning a foreign language or something comparable.

The points to emphasise when you go through pages 110-111 of the Student's Book with your class are:

1) Many language learners have reported that they benefited from reflecting in this way on their learning[9].

2) The diary entries can be in rough note form – there is no need to write in perfect sentences.

3) You will check after each of the first few units to see that students have written something in their diaries, but you will not actually read a student's diary unless he tells you he is willing for you to do so.

4) You will in any case be interested to discuss with individual students the ideas that come up in their diaries.

Monitor in the early stages of the course to ensure that all students attempt some kind of diary entry for each unit, but leave them to decide whether to hand their diaries in for you to read. If they hand their diaries in, respond to each entry in some way – by writing a few words at the bottom of the page, or by a chat with the individual at the end of a lesson. Another way of reinforcing the motivation of students to keep a Learner Diary is to feed some of the ideas or issues raised in their diaries back into class discussion; when you do this, select issues that you think will be of common interest and take care not to reveal the identity of the diarist(s) who originally wrote about them. If you operate a tutorial system, you can give your students the option of using their diary entries as a basis for discussion with their tutor.

Your response should certainly not focus on language errors made by students in writing their diaries; if you give the impression that the student's priority should be to produce error-free writing, you are likely to stifle communication and defeat the purpose of the exercise.

Before the next session

Establish with your students that this homework is necessary, not optional. If some students attend the next session without having completed the preparation tasks properly, they limit their own participation and learning, and may hinder the work of the rest of the class.

We recommend that you raise this important issue with your class early on in the course, and agree on a code of conduct with them: our classes have usually agreed that, if a student attends a session without having completed a specified preparation task, he should be required to complete it on his own during the session, while the rest of the class proceeds with the scheduled activities; one unprepared student should not be allowed to waste the time of the rest of the class.

MANAGING THE SPEAKING CLASS

To maximise the quantity and variety of speaking practice enjoyed by your students in the speaking class, you have to take each lesson through a sequence of stages or modes of interaction: for example, students working individually, students working together in pairs or groups, students working all together observed by the teacher, the teacher addressing the whole class. It is important in all but the last of these for the teacher actively to monitor the students as they practise, circulating from pair or group to group as appropriate. In this way she can assess, diagnose and select feedback to give to individual students and the class as a whole. If possible, the number of students in the class should be kept fairly small (12 to 16 is ideal) and the seating arrangements in the classroom should be flexible so as to allow smooth transitions from one mode to another.

If pair and group work tasks are set up well, most students find them motivating, particularly when they receive personalised feedback on their performance from the teacher. Help students to manage their own pair and group work effectively: make sure that the task and their goal are clear to them at the outset; encourage them to appoint a time-keeper for each group task, and, when appropriate, a secretary to take notes and a chairperson to ensure that everyone has the opportunity to contribute.

VISUAL AIDS

The effective use of visual aids is regarded as a fundamental presentation skill in most university departments, and so this course includes tasks to practise it. For these tasks you will need to provide either poster-sized sheets of paper (at least 400 cm by 600 cm) for display on the board, or transparencies (OHTs) for use with an overhead projector (OHP), and the appropriate pens.

Handouts are another standard feature of academic presentations, and they are therefore referred to in the **Preparing a presentation: prompt questions** on pages 115-117 of the Student's Book. However, as some of the teachers using this book will not have easy access to a photocopying machine, there are no tasks specifically concerned with handouts. If you are fortunate enough to have such access in your institution, do give your students the opportunity to practise producing and using handouts as part of the formal presentation tasks.

More sophisticated technology becomes available as an aid to presentation and discussion each year. In some institutions, for example, teachers and students are now able to display their visual aids by computer and incorporate multimedia material into their presentations. On the ideal EAP course, students would be given the opportunity to practise using the same types of equipment as they will subsequently need to use in their academic studies. In reality, whichever method of visual display you practise with your students, whether it is by poster or computer, the basic criteria of legibility and clarity remain the same.

HOMOGENEOUS AND MIXED CLASSES

The course can be used with both ethnically homogeneous (i.e. all from the same country or ethnic group) and mixed (i.e. from a number of different countries) classes. Most of the material is equally suitable for use with a class studying English in their own country, or with a class of international students from various countries studying in an English-speaking environment. At certain points in both the Student's and Teacher's Books, however, we have indicated how a particular task should be adapted for use with a class whose students are all from the same country.

LESSON PREPARATION

We recommend that before starting to teach a unit, you should read carefully through the *whole* unit in both the Student's Book and the Teacher's Book, to make sure that you understand the purpose of each session within the unit, and what your preparation needs to include. Essential preparation may involve familiarising yourself with reading or listening texts, or preparing to give a presentation of your own, as well as ensuring that you have the necessary aids available for yourself and your students to use – blank posters or OHTs, cassette player and cassettes, etc.

Notes

1. International English Language Testing System. Many universities now require international students to achieve a score of at least 6.5 on the IELTS scale before they start their academic courses.

2. Test of English as a Foreign Language.

3. For simplicity and clarity only, the learner is referred to as 'he' and the teacher as 'she' throughout this book.

4 English for Academic Purposes.

5. See Clare Furneaux *et al*, 'Talking heads and shifting bottoms' in P. Adams, Heaton and Howarth (eds), (1991) *Sociocultural Issues in EAP*, Prentice Hall ELT, for discussion of the different types of seminar that are common on UK university courses.

6. Helen Johnson, 'Defossilising', *ELT Journal*, 46/2 (April 1992) p.180

7. See Tom Hutchinson and Alan Waters, (1987) *English for Specific Purposes*, CUP, pp.56-8, for the distinction between the learner's needs and lacks.

8. Except in Unit 10 (see page 77)

9. For a list of references, see Kathleen M. Bailey, 'The use of diary studies in teacher education programmes' in Jack C. Richards and David Nunan (eds), (1990) *Second Language Teacher Education*, CUP.

USING FEEDBACK NOTES

An efficient way of giving individualised feedback when your class is carrying out an oral communication task is as follows: mark four sections on a sheet of note-paper (see illustration below) and then, as you observe the performance of individual students, record your feedback under the appropriate headings. When selecting points to give feedback on, bear in mind the principles for **Giving feedback effectively** listed on page 122 of the Student's Book.

At the end of the task, give the feedback note to the student as a basis for remedial work and a useful reminder when preparing for later tasks. If you have access to carbon paper or a photocopying machine, you can retain a copy of the feedback notes for your file. In any case, you should keep a record of the number of feedback notes you give each student, to ensure that everyone receives their fair share during the course.

If you use these feedback notes with your students regularly, you will be able to establish your own conventions for indicating errors and corrections quickly and easily. With some students' errors of grammar and vocabulary, it may be enough to write down what the student said and then leave him to identify the error and how to correct it; of course, you would need to follow this kind of feedback up later by checking that he had successfully corrected the error. In other cases, it may be appropriate to include in your feedback some specific remedial action – for example, by stating the relevant page in a reference grammar.

If pronunciation is a problem area for your students, you need to establish with them a set of symbols you can use to represent phonemes and syllable stress – one option is to adopt the symbols used in the English–English dictionary you recommend to your students (e.g. *Oxford Advanced Learners' Dictionary*).

STUDENT'S NAME: Vocabulary	DATE: Pronunciation
Grammar	Skill/Other

The feedback notes are even more beneficial to the student if you are able to audio-record his performance and then give him the recording and your feedback note together.

The kind of error you choose to highlight will naturally depend on the strengths and weaknesses of your particular students. One possible example of a completed feedback note is given below.

STUDENT'S NAME: Sam	DATE: 15/7/97
Vocabulary	Pronunciation
1 balance of payment *deficiency* 2 standard of *life* 3 vicious circle ≠ virtuous circle	1 project/dz/not/z/ 2 'sensible 3 The main 'exports are …
Grammar	Skill/Other
1. 'If the domestic economy will be opened to international competition it would have declined.' (see Murphy, p.72) 2. 'In spite this problem, ….' (see Murphy, p.128)	1. An overview would have helped us to follow your presentation. 2. Not enough eye contact with audience. 3. Write important figures and

FOUNDATION UNIT: YOU AND YOUR COURSE

You need to prepare: cassette player(s) and cassette(s) for Task 3.3.

SESSION 1

As in any short, intensive course, the teaching of the opening unit is particularly important in setting the tone and establishing standards for the course as a whole.

Step 1: Listening [5m]

1.1 This is an opportunity for you to introduce yourself to your students. Prepare by deciding which of the topic areas listed in the Student's Book you are going to say something about and in which order. Bear in mind that the way in which you give your talk here will inevitably be taken as something of a model by your students when they come to perform Task 1.3.

Step 2: Introducing yourself [15m]

1.2 Tell students that, when selecting topic areas to talk about, they should ask themselves what their audience is likely to find most interesting. Tell them how long you want them to spend on these activities: two minutes to prepare, followed (in Task 1.3) by three minutes for each speaker is usually about right.

When they have had time to decide on their topic areas, ask them to turn to **Repair expressions** on page 139 in the Language Help section. As this is the first time they have used the Language Help section, explain that the page lists some expressions that may be useful in the task to come. Go through the expressions with the class, and for each one:

- Model the pronunciation, and drill as appropriate for your class.
- Elicit/establish how it is used, including an example in context.

1.3 Get students into groups of three or four. If some students already know each other, or have similar backgrounds, separate them into different groups as far as possible.

Step 3: Discussion and reporting back [20m]

1.4 and 1.5

This is an opportunity for you to learn about the students' existing attitudes and to suggest and explain alternatives where appropriate. Your contribution to the class discussion will depend on the comments of your particular students. You may find some of the following points, which were raised by teachers during the trialling of the materials, relevant to your own class discussion:

a) A 'perfect native-speaker accent' is not necessary for successful study in English – many thousands of international students have completed degree courses without one. An attribute that is necessary, however, is the ability to communicate meaning precisely on a range of subjects without placing undue strain on the listener. Learners need to monitor their pronunciation and seek feedback from the people they speak to, in order to identify the features of their English pronunciation that place strain on the listener or otherwise impede communication. Some learners, for example, will find that it is errors in word stress or intonation, rather than individual sounds, that cause difficulties for the listener.

b) As in a) above, formal accuracy is only one aspect of competence and does not need to be perfect. Nevertheless, the learner certainly does need to acquire a high degree of control over morphology, sentence structure and the use of cohesive devices, in order to be able to communicate meaning precisely and with ease on a range of subjects.

c) Vocabulary expansion is certainly one of the keys for language learners to improving their ease, precision and range of expression. (You may want to discuss with your students what learning vocabulary involves: When do you feel you 'know' a new item? Why is it not simply a question of memorising word-lists? etc.)

   As well as expanding their vocabulary, EAP learners should also practise strategies, such as paraphrasing or exemplification, to enable them to cope when they do not know or cannot remember a particular word.

e) Extensive reading may improve the learner's knowledge of vocabulary and grammar, and the improved knowledge can then be drawn on in oral communication. However, learners who read extensively in English without hearing it spoken are likely to form some incorrect ideas about and habits of pronunciation. Their oral fluency may also be hampered by a mistaken belief that they have to reproduce in speech the very tightly structured English of written text. (See Ronald Carter and Michael McCarthey 'Grammar and the Spoken Language' in *Applied Linguistics* Vol. 16, 2 (1995), for a discussion of the distinctive structure of spoken English.)

f) The kind of practice described is certainly likely to improve the learner's fluency, and probably his confidence. To avoid settling into a 'fluent but fossilised' state, he needs to monitor how precisely and over how wide a range of topics he is communicating.

g) Learners need various kinds of practice so as to develop the various aspects of competence, giving priority to language accuracy at certain times and to communication at others. Perhaps the learner quoted here should adjust the balance between the two, by setting a target for the proportion of practice time during which he will deliberately 'switch the language monitor off' and concentrate on communication (see also b) above).

h) Many colleges and universities have a large number of international students, and so EAP learners need to get used to working in English with peers from a range of language backgrounds. For discussion and presentation practice (where the focus is on communication or skill rather than formal accuracy), pair work and group work provide a more authentic context than when the teacher interacts with individual students briefly in turn. Pair work and group work also greatly increase the amount of oral communication practice available to each member of the class. Because the teacher can circulate and observe the pairs and groups at work, she is still able to correct errors when appropriate. (This is an opportunity for you to explain the policy you intend to follow on correction of language errors.)

At the end of the class discussion draw students' attention to the six points in the section headed 'How to get the most out of the course' on pages ix-x of the Student's Book:

- Think about your learning.
- Think, plan and rehearse for tasks.
- Seek and make use of feedback on your performance.
- Be an active listener and speaker.
- Keep your language records up to date.
- Make use of language reference books.

From time to time during the course, give students feedback on their approach to learning by referring them specifically to items in this list which they are either neglecting or carrying out successfully.

Step 4: Before the next session

1.6   The purpose of the Learner Questionnaire is to help the learner identify his lacks, and set goals for his learning. It is one of the items in this course which are designed to promote independent learning by the students. See page xi for a note on the principle of independent learning.

Quickly go through Part 1 of the Learner Questionnaire with the students, explaining anything that you think might otherwise cause confusion. Explain to them that each individual student must do this homework task in order to be properly prepared for the next session, when it will be discussed.

SESSION 2

Step 1: Preparation [3m]

2.1 The overall purpose of Steps 1 to 3 here is to make students aware of the value of using certain strategies when exchanging information in a foreign language. For this reason, students are deliberately given very little help in advance with Task 2.1.

The two diagrams are on page 71 and page 74 of the Student's Book. Give students a time limit to work to: say two minutes to prepare and then (in Task 2.2) three minutes each way to exchange information.

Step 2: Information exchange and discussion [7m]

2.2 See page xiv for a note on this type of task. Monitor, noting examples of the strategies being used effectively, and of an exchange being inefficient because of the failure to use them. Keep your interventions to a minimum on this occasion.

2.3 This is of course a matter of personal opinion. Examples of acceptable answers given during trialling are:

'The fact that the proportion of overseas students at postgraduate level is generally so high.'

'The fact that the 'female subjects' at this UK university seem to be very much the same as at the universities in my country and my partner's country.'

Step 3: Review [10m]

See page xv for a note on this type of activity.

2.4 Check students' answers to these questions. In answer to the second question, try to elicit from the class some strategies along the lines of those listed in 2.5.

2.5 Before students try to answer the questions, go through the checklist with your class and elucidate as necessary for them.

The extract below illustrates the use of some of the strategies for exchanging information efficiently that are listed on page 3 (Student's Book). For instance, the two speakers start by discussing how to carry out the task – they decide on a procedure. Then, when Speaker B starts to summarise the information in his diagram, he gives a general description of it first before going into more specific detail; in other words he frames the information, and it is noticeable that Speaker A later follows the same kind of practice.

A: Okay, I've looked at my diagram. Now, how shall we do this?

B: Shall I tell you about my diagram first? Then you can ask questions if you want, and then go on to talk about your own diagram.

A: That sounds fine to me.

B: Okay. I've got a chart. It shows the number of male and female students in each faculty at Reading University in the UK in 1996-97. There are five faculties shown – Social Science, Science, Agriculture, Engineering and Education. For each of these, the chart shows the numbers of male and female students. In two of the faculties the females outnumber the males by a long way...

A: Can I just check: are your figures for postgraduate students only?

B: No, I don't think so. Let me see. It says, 'Figures for all full-time students at the University of Reading', so it must include both graduates and undergraduates.

A: Right, thanks. Now, where were we?

B: I was saying that the women outnumber the men by almost three to one in the case of Education, and by about two to one in Social Science, which is the biggest of the five faculties. I can give you specific figures if you want, but I'd be interested to hear what kind of information you've got.

A: All right. My diagram covers the same year as yours, and it also shows student numbers by faculty, but this time they are broken down into home and international students. Oh, and the information in my chart is about postgraduate students only.

B: It's Reading University again, is it?

A: Yes, it is, with the same five faculties as yours...

Step 4: Exchange and discussion [15m]

2.6 The purpose of this task is three-fold: it provides an opportunity for students to practise some of the strategies they discussed in the previous task; it raises their awareness of what their EAP learning needs are; and it orientates them to the subject matter of the extended listening task in Session 3.

When the groups have had time to discuss the questions, have a round-up in which the whole class hears from each group. Draw out students' various ideas about the kinds of oral task they will have to perform on their academic courses.

SESSION 3

The central task in this session is a jigsaw listening – see page xiv for a note on how to conduct this type of task.

Step 1: Preparing to listen [6m]

3.1 This is intended to be a rapid, teacher-led discussion, to serve as a warm-up for the main listening task.

3.2 When you elicit questions from the class, steer them towards the kind of subject matter that is actually dealt with in the listening text. You could draw up on the board a list or map of the most interesting, relevant questions for discussion after the listening tasks.

Step 2: Listening and checking [20m]

3.3   Go through the worksheet with students and elucidate as necessary. During the first listening (tapescript on pages 83–87 of Student's Book) students should make notes on a separate sheet, not on the worksheet (see page 7 for completed worksheet).

3.4   Circulate, monitoring each group's discussion, to ensure that it is on the right lines. If a major misunderstanding persists, correct it at this stage so as to prevent it from being transmitted to other students in tasks that follow.

Step 3: Information exchange and discussion [20m]

3.5   Point out that some of the strategies for exchanging information, which were discussed earlier in this unit (Task 2.5), may be useful in carrying out this task.

3.6   When students in pairs or small groups have had time to discuss these questions, ask them to report back to the class. This gives you the opportunity to check on students' understanding of the different kinds of oral communication task that are mentioned in the listening texts, and to clarify where necessary.

Step 4: Language review [15m]

See page xv for a note on this type of task, which occurs at the end of each unit. On this first occasion, it is worth devoting time in class to going carefully through the task.

3.7   Refer students to the **Repair expressions** on page 139 in the Language Help section, and ask whether they found these expressions helpful during tasks in this unit (e.g. Tasks 1.3 and 3.5). Elicit at least one or two expressions to add to this page by asking students to think of expressions which they wanted to use in Task 1.3 or similar tasks, but were unsure of. Demonstrate how expressions should be added to the Language Help section page (i.e. indicating clearly how the new expressions relate to the existing ones, with headings, explanations and examples where appropriate).

3.8   If time allows, do this task by copying the beginnings of the vocabulary map onto the board (or poster or OHT) and then eliciting from the class suggestions as to how it can be extended. Although there is no single 'right answer' for this kind of task, one possible version of the map is shown as an example on page 8.

Step 5: Before the next session

3.9   As mentioned above, the Learner Questionnaire is one of the items in this course which are designed to promote independent learning by the students. (See page xi for a note on the principle of independent learning.) Ensure that the independent learning process is set in motion from this very first unit, by making a point over the next few days of seeing each of your students individually, to check on and discuss their responses to the Learner Questionnaire (and, optionally, to the Learner Diary task as well).

LISTENING WORKSHEET (Foundation Unit, Task 3.3)

	Text 1	Text 2
1. What is the name of the person interviewed?	John Mitchell	Dr Catherine Andrews
2. Which course/department is he/she involved in?	Construction Management (MSc)	Tropical Agricultural Development (MSc)
3. How many international students are there?	About $\frac{3}{4}$ are overseas	40 overseas (10 UG and 30 PG)
4. Does he/she find that the international students have a lot of language problems?	Very few problems	On the whole, no. But difficulty in following lectures is the most common problem.
5. For what purpose do students need to be able to communicate well orally?	a) computer simulation ('Arousal') b) initial discussion of 3 essay topics with tutor c) case studies d) making a film e) on-site project	a) understanding lectures and stating own opinion/problem b) seminars: S gives presentation to rest of group c) tutorials d) assessment e) case studies
6. What advice does he/she give international students?	a) 'Above all, mix.' Important for Ss to mix widely, with other Ss and staff. Avoid congregating in small ethnic groups.	a) Recognise that the style of teaching is not very formal and that the students are invited/expected to contribute. b) Take advantage of opportunity for informal contact with colleagues: social activities in the department can help you to become comfortable with English. c) Tell tutor if you have a language problem – don't hide it. Staff will be sympathetic.

LEARNER DIARY ONE

See page xvi for a detailed note on this type of task, which occurs at the end of each unit. As this is the first Learner Diary task in the course, go through the questions in class and check that the students understand what they are expected to do.

Make a particular effort to respond to students' entries for this first Learner Diary. You may well find that some students raise issues that would be of common interest or value to the class; if so, feed these issues back into class discussion at the first appropriate opportunity, without revealing the identity of the student(s) who raised them.

SHEET A

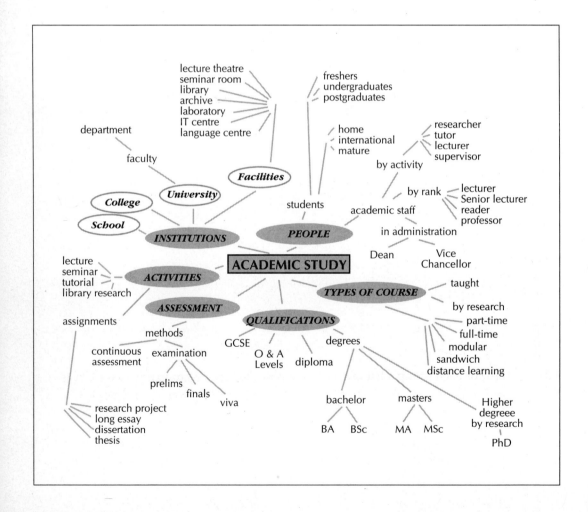

UNIT

1

COUNTRIES

SKILLS FOCUS: Preparing a presentation

You need to prepare: master question list collated by teacher for Task 2.1; copies of examples of visual aids on page 18 and page 19 for Task 2.3; blank OHTs or large sheets of paper, and pens, for Task 2.5.

SESSION 1

Step 1: Exploring the topic [8m]

1.1   In this task, students practise one way of beginning to explore a topic for a presentation, by making an ideas map. The ideas map technique is intended to help the user clarify relations between ideas, identify gaps in his thinking, and generate further ideas. The best way to conduct this task, particularly if your students are not familiar with the concept of ideas maps, is probably for you to build the map up on the board by eliciting suggestions from the class.

1.2   This is intended to be a quick exchange of ideas; monitor to ensure that students do not get bogged down in too much detail.

Step 2: Preparing to collect information [8m]

1.3   Monitor each group's list of questions: point out to the group any cases where the meaning of a question is not clear. If necessary, help groups to think of suitable sub-topic headings.

Step 3: Language focus [18m]

1.4   See page xiv for a note on how to conduct this type of task. Go through the expressions for **Asking questions after a presentation** with your students, modelling and drilling as necessary.

1.5   If you are from the same country as your students, the topic of your presentation could be either the English-speaking country you know best, or some aspect of it, or the district or region you come from within your country.

If you are teaching a mixed class of international students in an English-speaking country, the topic should be a perspective on that country which you think will be of interest to your particular students. During the trialling of these materials in the UK, the topics selected by teachers and approved of by students included 'Britain and Ireland', 'The disunited United Kingdom' and 'Is the UK part of Europe?'

Your presentation, which you need to prepare thoroughly in advance of this session, should have the same time limit (6m) as your students will face later in the unit. The presentation you give here will inevitably be taken as something of an example by your students when they come to perform a similar task later in the unit. So, take the opportunity to model as far as possible the good practice that you want them to follow, particularly with regard to the points raised in **Assessing Presentations: Checklist 1** which is introduced later in this unit (Student's Book page 112)

- Plan – think about what your audience would find interesting and/or useful
    - think about how much you can cover in the time available
    - decide on headings to organise the content of your talk
- Speak clearly and expressively, at an appropriate pace and volume.
- Do not read from a script; use headings and, if necessary, brief notes.
- Help the audience to recognise the structure of your talk:
    - give a quick overview at the beginning
    - indicate when you move from one section to the next.
- Distribute eye contact evenly.
- Keep to your time limit

Allow at least four or five minutes for questions after the presentation: in order to encourage students to form their questions with some care, you may want to tell them that you will only answer questions which are formed correctly.

Step 4: Extending your ideas map [3m]

At the end of Session 1

Remember to collect from each group the question list they compiled in Task 1.3.

Before Session 2

You need to collate the question lists, to produce from them a master question list divided into three sections (headed, for example, Geography, Economy, Culture) with roughly the same number of questions in each. You need a copy of this master list for each researcher to use in Task 2.2 (see page 11).

Example of master question list collated by teacher at end of Session 1 for use in Session 2

Geography

Where is country X located?

What are its neighbouring countries?

What are its main topographical features?

What type of climate does it have?

Does it divide up naturally into regions?

Economy

Who are country X's principal trading partners?

What are is main industries?

What are the main imports and exports?

What proportion of the workforce is engaged in agriculture?

Which sectors of the economy are currently creating new jobs?

Culture

What, if anything, is distinctive about the culture of country X?

What do people regard as its most important traditions?

Are these in fact still commonly practised?

What are the most noticeable or significant changes that have taken place in recent years?

SESSION 2

Step 1: Collecting information [20m]

2.1   Divide the class into groups of four, ensuring as far as possible that there are students from a number of different countries (or different districts, if all your students are from the same country) within each group. In each group of four appoint:

a) one informant, whose role is to answer questions about his country (or district) of origin. Select as informants students from a number of different countries (or districts). You may need to prompt the informants as to what kinds of language are likely to be relevant.

b) three researchers, whose role is to ask questions to obtain information in preparation for a presentation about the informant's country (or district). In each group, assign the three sections of the question list to the three researchers, so that each researcher prepares to ask a different set of questions. Remind the researchers that they will have just five minutes each to collect their information; tell them to time one another so that they can prevent anyone from taking up time that is due to the next person.

Step 2: Drafting an outline [12m]

2.2 Explain that in Session 3 each group of students will tell the class about its informant's country (or district), as clearly and interestingly as possible. The six questions given here for discussion are intended to help the groups decide on the content of their presentation. Tell students that at the end of this discussion you want to see a simple outline of what they are going to talk about in their presentation, consisting of the major points listed in order. Draw their attention to the fact that they will have a maximum of six minutes to give the presentation, and establish that this time limit is to be strictly observed and will be enforced by guillotine if necessary.

The tasks in this session deliberately separate drafting an outline (in Step 2, where students sort out what they are going to talk about, i.e. they decide on content) from drafting aids (in Step 4, where they produce something for display to the audience), in order to ensure that both steps receive due attention. Otherwise, if this separation is not made, some students may rush to produce an outline for display before they have properly thought through the content of their presentation.

Step 3: Discussion – using aids [10m]

2.3 Later in the unit, and then throughout the course, students will need to produce simple visual aids for use in their own presentations. This task is therefore intended to get students to think about when they should use visual aids, and what features they should incorporate in their visual aids. You need to reproduce (on the board, or a poster, or an OHT, or a photocopied handout) the two examples given on page 18 and page 19, for display to your students in question 2).

Notes and possible answers to the questions

1) Because it is the most efficient way of conveying certain kinds of information.
   It can make information easier to understand and/or to remember.
   It allows continual reference by the audience.
   The visual stimulus lends variety and interest to the presentation.

2) The second of the two displays the outline much more effectively. Most of the dos and don'ts listed below are illustrated by one or other of the display outlines.

3) **DO**

   • Write clearly and neatly.

   • Include a title.

   • Make use of layout, underlining, numbering, and variation of lettering.

   • Keep the number of words to a minimum, using key words as far as possible.

   • Use pictures/symbols/etc. where appropriate (it is a *visual* aid).

DON'T

   • Do not write too small.

- Do not overload it with detail (the more crowded it is, the less impressive each point).
- Do not use it to present extended text (a handout is more appropriate for this).

4) To save the audience from having to take notes, so that they can concentrate on listening to you.

For a worksheet or a particularly long or detailed text that you want the audience to refer to during the presentation.

For additional reading for the audience to take away at the end of the presentation.

Step 4: Drafting aids (12m)

2.4 Here the group discusses and then (in 2.5) produces the aids it will use in its presentation in Session 3. We recommend that all groups should produce a display outline (question 1) and a prompt sheet (question 4). You need to provide either large, blank sheets of paper (A3 size at least), or OHTs, and pens.

Notes on the questions

1) If they produced a good, clear outline in Task 2.2 above, it may simply be a question of transferring headings from there to the visual aid. You could set a maximum word limit (of say, 20 words), to encourage students to practise the use of key words.

2) For a presentation about a foreign country, other visual aids that immediately come to mind are: map of the country; illustrative pictures of landscape, architecture, costume, etc.

3) The preparation of a handout tends to be time-consuming and linguistically demanding. At this early stage in the course, therefore, especially with relatively weak classes, it is probably better to steer them away from producing a handout. If they do want to use a handout, arrange to vet a draft of it *before* multiple copies are made.

4) Because of the difficulty of presenting in a foreign language, some students will want to read word-for-word from a script when they are presenting. Emphasise that this is not acceptable, as it prevents the speaker from having eye contact with the audience, and that they must therefore practise using reduced notes on prompt cards or a prompt sheet. Rehearsal will be very important for these students.

Step 5: Before the next class

2.6 It is probably best, at this early stage in the course, for you to appoint the presenter in each group; choose someone who is fairly confident and who you think will manage the task well.

2.7 Arrange for the presenters to practise using the OHP, if necessary.

SESSION 3

Step 1: Discussion [6m]

3.1 The purpose of this task is for the class to establish some basic criteria for assessing the effectiveness of a presentation. Spend a few minutes eliciting, and developing on the board, a list of criteria along the lines of those reflected in **Assessing Presentations: Checklists 1 and 2** in the Independent Learner section (pages 112-113). The process of eliciting is valuable here: it enables you to gauge your students' awareness of the criteria involved; and it is likely to give the students a sense of 'ownership' of the criteria and, by extension, of the procedure that will be used in peer and self-evaluation throughout the course.

Having elicited and discussed some criteria, direct students to **Assessing Presentations: Checklist 1** (page 112) and explain that it incorporates the most important criteria in the form of a checklist, for use as an aide memoire by the individual learner and as a means of peer feedback in class. Quickly go through **Checklist 1** with the class, so that they are ready to use it in Task 3.3 below.

Step 2: Giving a presentation [9m = 6m for presentation + 3m for questions]

3.2 Remind the class that you intend to guillotine any presentation that exceeds its allotted time.

- During the presentation, prepare a feedback note along the lines shown on page xx. Your note should certainly include feedback on the main language errors, as they will not be dealt with in peer feedback.

- If possible, audio-record each group's presentation on a separate cassette. At the end of the lesson you will then be able to give each group a recording of its presentation and a feedback note about it.

Step 3: Preparing feedback [5m]

3.3 Later in the session, you will want students to hand their feedback on to the groups concerned, so at this stage you need either to provide each student with two or three photocopies of the blank checklist, or to ask students to note down their feedback on an ordinary sheet of paper by clearly numbering their answers to the checklist questions, as follows:

Feedback on Group 1's presentation	
1.	Yes
2.	A little
3.	Quite
4.	
5a.	etc.

Monitor to make sure that groups are producing helpful, constructive feedback, particularly in response to question 7, which is open-ended and therefore more difficult to deal with.

Step 4: Repeat for other groups [36m = 9m for each of 4 groups]

3.4 You need to enforce the time limits strictly here so as to allow time for all groups to give their presentation and receive feedback. Guillotining an overlong presentation gives a clear message to the presenters that they need to pay more attention to timing in their next presentation, and may also save the audience from getting bored.

Step 5: Exchanging feedback [10m]

3.5 Ensure the 'feedback groups' for this task contain one member of each 'presentation group' from previous tasks, so that there is someone to explain feedback notes if necessary.

You may want to refer students to the principles for Giving feedback effectively on page 122 of the Student's Book. In any case, monitor to ensure that the feedback is given constructively.

3.6 In other words, decide:

1) Which group gave the most interesting presentation?
2) Which group/speaker helped you most effectively to follow the main points?
3) Which group made the best use of visual aids? etc.

Step 6: Language review [12m]

See page xv for a note on how to conduct this type of task.

3.7 Refer students to **Asking questions after a presentation** on page 127 in the Language Help section, and ask if they found these expressions helpful when the other groups gave their presentations in Session 3.

3.8 If time allows, do this task by copying the beginnings of the vocabulary map onto the board and then eliciting from the class suggestions as to how it can be extended. One possible version of the map is shown as an example on page 17, but there is of course no single 'right answer' for this kind of task.

Step 7: Before the next session

3.9 (If it was not possible for you to record the presentations as recommended in 3.2 above, omit this task.)

Discuss with students the value of listening to a recording of their presentation. Give each presentation group your feedback note and the recording of their presentation. Explain that each student in this group should read the feedback note and listen to the recording in the next day or two.

3.10   Direct students to the model for **Preparing a presentation** on page 114. Point out that in the course of this unit they have gone through the four phases, and also most of the 12 steps and prompt questions, which are listed there.

The purpose of this model is two-fold:

- to stimulate discussion and raise awareness of what preparing a presentation involves

- to serve as a practical aid throughout the course for those students whose previous experience of preparing a presentation even in their own language was very limited.

We hope that the model reflects good practice, but the intention is certainly not to prescribe one correct procedure for all students in all circumstances.

LEARNER DIARY TWO

See page xvi for a detailed note on how to conduct this type of task. As this is only the second Learner Diary task in the course, go through the questions in class and check that the students understand what they are expected to do. You may also be able to make some brief, general comment on the entries that students wrote for Learner Diary One.

SHEET B

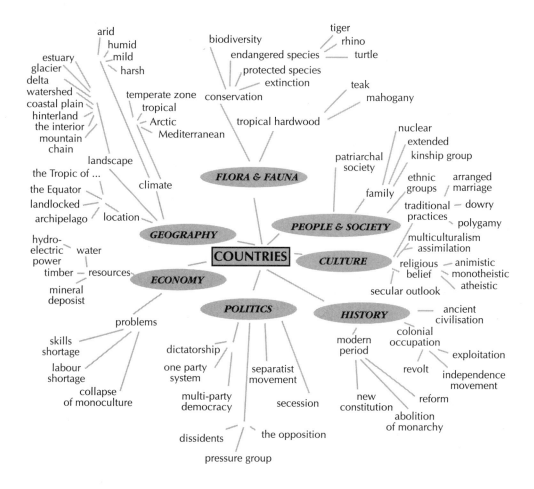

EXAMPLE 1

Wales is located to the west of Central England. To its west are the Atlantic Ocean and the Irish Sea, which separates it from the island of Ireland 50 miles away. An upland region, like the West of Scotland and the North-West of England, with relatively heavy rainfall. The population (2.9 million in 1992) is concentrated in the valleys and coastal strip of South Wales.

This region industrialised rapidly after 1800. The coal, steel and shipbuilding industries all prospered during the nineteenth century, but have declined in recent decades. Now, after a period of very high unemployment, hopes are pinned on the micro-electronic firms established in the last 20 years, many with investment from the Pacific Rim.

The earliest records we have of Wales being governed as a political and legal entity are from the time of King Hywel the Good (died 950). However, the border between the Welsh and English kingdoms was continually fought over. The powerful English king Edward I invaded in 1282 and reduced most of Wales to the status of a principality. The Act of Union of 1535 united the two countries and Wales has remained part of the United Kingdom to the present day. Separatist sentiment is not as strong as in some other parts of the UK: of the 36 MPs representing Welsh constituencies following the 1992 election, only 8 are WNP (5 Conservative, 23 Labour).

As in other countries, the distinctiveness of the local culture has diminished in Wales as a result of modern, international communications. Nevertheless, the number of Welsh speakers has grown steadily since 1970 (they now amount to 20% of the population), and the Welsh language TV service is flourishing. Traditional poetry and song feature much more prominently in popular culture in Wales than in England. The annual Eisteddfod festival still attracts participants from all over the country.

EXAMPLE 2

AN INTRODUCTION TO WALES

1. **GEOGRAPHY**
   - location
   - population
   - economy   - C19 coal and steel

                      - C21 micro-electronics?

2. **POLITICAL HISTORY**
   - Hywel the Good, first King of Wales (d. 950)
   - Principality 1282
   - Act of Union 1535
   - WNP 26% 1992

3. **A NATIONAL IDENTITY?**
   - Welsh language
   - poetry and song (annual Eisteddfod)
   - hwyl and hyraeth
   - rugby

UNIT
2

THE HOME

SKILLS FOCUS: Preparing for your audience

You need to prepare: a brief description of a home you have lived in for 1.1, answers to questions in 1.4.

SESSION 1

Step 1: Warm-up/Discussion [5m]

1.1   This is a quick, introductory activity to start students thinking about the topic. Give an example of a home you have lived in. Examples of discussion points here:

- lower-level students: location, size, rooms
- higher-level students: atmosphere, reasons for liking or disliking a particular home, reasons for living in a particular home.

Step 2: Collecting information [35m]

1.2   Give the students two minutes to note down as many questions as they can think of. Possible additional questions:

- Who pays for it?
- What is inside it?
- What work is done in the home?
- What animals live/are allowed in it?

1.3   Elicit questions from the ones written down and, as a class, agree on the most interesting two questions for everyone to add to their questionnaire under questions 5 and 6.

1.4   If you are familiar with homes in Britain, answer these questions from your own knowledge. If you are not, use the listening text 'The home in Britain' on the tape (tapescript on pages 88-89 in the Student's Book), which answers questions 1–4 with the following information:

1) one person
   married couples with no children
   families with children at home
   single parents with children
   unrelated adults sharing
   extended families
2) rent
   a deposit plus a mortgage from a bank or building society
3) milkman
   newspaper boy or girl
   postman
   door-to-door salesmen
   people collecting for charity
   window cleaner
   burglars
   doctor
   home-helps
   district nurses
   friends and relatives
4) birthday parties
   dinner parties
   wedding receptions
   food and drink after a funeral
   friends calling for a special activity, e.g. playing cards (bridge), watching a
   special football match, getting a take-away meal and a video

1.5   Monitor the students and help with vocabulary where necessary.

If all your students are from the same country, establish now what district each person will focus on in this unit. If they come from different parts of the country, districts will be regions, cities, towns or villages. If they come from the same part, districts will be suburbs, neighbourhoods or even streets within the area.

Step 3: Preparing for your audience [10m]

1.6   Noting down answers to the questions here is an important activity; its purpose is to encourage students to think about their audience before they decide what to say in a talk. Having identified what the audience already knows about the topic, students should focus their talk on what will be new and interesting for the audience.

If the class is mixed with some people from the same country/district, tell the students to prepare their talk for the part of the audience that is from a different country/district (the others can check that they are correct!).

Give an example of answers to the questions, e.g. for Britain:

1) very little: he may think that houses are big and made of bricks (from TV programmes showing rich people);

2) variety – houses, flats, mobile homes; cost; how we pay for a home; who lives there; gardens and gardening;

3) each child, ideally, has his own room; an increasing number of people now work from home, instead of going in to an office to work (communications at home: computers, fax machines).

At the end of Session 1

Tell the students to prepare a two-minute talk for Session 2 on the home in their country/district, using some of the information from 1.5 and 1.6. Remind them that two minutes is not very long and that, before Session 2, they should time themselves giving their talk and shorten it if necessary.

SESSION 2

Step 1: Giving short talks [50m]

2.1 Put the students into suitable pairings, ensuring as far as possible that people from the same country/district are not working together.

2.2 Explain the procedure for this activity carefully. Begin by explaining the instructions you will use:

- recap the speaker's last point
- contradict the speaker's last point
- summarise what the speaker has said so far
- ask for more information about one of the speaker's points
- predict the speaker's next point.

Present or remind students of useful language, e.g.

'To recap that last point, …'

'No, I don't agree with you when you say …'

'So, to summarise so far, …'

'In other words, …'

'Could you expand a little on what you said about …?'

'Are you going on to talk about …?'

See also **Repair expressions** (Student's Book page 139) and **Asking for clarification** (Student's Book page 126) in the Language Help section.

During the talks, stop the whole class and ask the listeners in each pair to carry out one of the above instructions. After 30 seconds, ask the speakers to continue until you stop them again with another instruction. How many times you interrupt in this way depends on the level of your class, but do it at least twice.

Stop the activity after the speakers have had about two minutes of speaking time (excluding the time following your instructions).

The primary aims here are to give students practice (as speakers) in producing a well-structured long turn, and (as listeners) in recognising and using its structure in order to listen more effectively.

2.3 Be strict with time keeping.

2.4 Again, strict time keeping is important.

2.5 Select, or ask the class to nominate, two students to give an expanded version of their talk (a five-minute presentation) to the whole group.

2.6 Do this orally and write the two points agreed to on the board. Refer the class back to the questions in 1.6. Things to remember here might include:

- it is a mixed audience: some people know quite a lot about the home in this country/district, some know very little
- everyone is interested in why people choose to live there
- nobody knows about the cost of homes there.

Step 2: Before the next session

2.7 Tell students studying in Britain to find answers to the quiz from other students, local people or from their own observations. Students who cannot do this should focus on question 6.

2.8 Tell students to bring to the next class any typical items from the home in their country, or pictures of them. Read Step 3 on pages 19-20 in the Student's Book and refer students to 3.8 so they know what they will do with this topic in class. Items could include eating utensils (e.g. chopsticks, cutlery, bowls, plates), cooking utensils (e.g. cooking/coffee pots, special knives, vegetable peelers, pestle and mortars), other household objects (e.g. lamps, bedding), religious implements. If students find it difficult to think of such utilitarian items, they could include any items they would take with them to remind them of home (e.g. picture, holiday souvenir, favourite ornament).

2.9 Remind the two presenters of the importance of preparation, e.g. clear OHTs, practising to get the timing right for their talks.

Session 3

Step 1: Checking the quiz [5m]

3.1 Go over the answers to the quiz (see page 24), briefly explaining any interesting points.

Step 2: Giving presentations [20m]

3.2 Stop any talk that exceeds the five-minute time limit.

3.3 Students can give feedback by noting down the numbers from the 'Audience Feedback' printed in their book and writing their answers on a piece of paper. You may choose to let students complete the feedback in pairs.

3.4 As for 3.2 and 3.3.

Quiz: The Home in Britain – possible answers

1. Find the names of two houses.

   Homes can be named according to factors such as: physical characteristics (e.g. 'Fairview', 'Oak Tree Cottage', 'Mile End'), their previous/present function (e.g. The Vicarage, The Stables, The Mill), wishful thinking (e.g. 'The Retreat', 'The Nest'), someone's joke (e.g. 'Ywurrie' – say it aloud!).

2. What is an allotment?

   A piece of land in the town, rented for a small fee from the local council, on which plants (e.g. vegetables, flowers) are grown for personal consumption.

3. Find three different kinds of home on your route to class from where you are staying.

   e.g. detached, semi-detached, bungalow, terraced, flat, bedsit.

4. Find three different things people can have in their garden (apart from plants!).

   e.g. furniture: (tables, benches, chairs), barbecue, fishpond, birdtable, sandpit, swings, climbing frame, goalposts, sundial, greenhouse, garage, shed, washing line, gnome, statue, fountain, dustbins.

5. Complete the following English proverbs:

   a) 'An Englishman's home *is his castle.*'

   b) 'Home is where *the heart is.*'

   c) '*North, east, south, west,* home's best.'

6. *Proverbs from the students' mother tongue translated into English can be displayed on a notice board.*

3.5 Collect in all the written feedback and give it to both speakers to look at. You should comment on positive aspects of their presentations.

3.6 Ask students to note down two pieces of advice each. Elicit advice first from the two speakers from 3.2 and 3.4 and then from the whole class. Add your own points at the end if anything important has not been mentioned by the students. Make sure all students note down the advice. Points that should be made include:

- think of what your audience knows/does not know about your topic as you prepare your presentation; refer briefly to the former, focus on the latter
- speak clearly
- look at your audience and don't focus on one or two individuals
- signpost your talk clearly: say what you are going to talk about at the beginning, divide the talk up into clearly defined sections, make changes in topic obvious
- put key/difficult words on an OHT or the board and explain them
- mention things you know will interest your audience – make connections, where possible, with their experience

- do not read your talk
- have a definite conclusion – don't just stop.

Step 3: Describing and explaining [60m]

3.7 1) Possible answers:

- A pencil is a tool for writing with. It consists of two parts: a wooden, outer part and a middle part made of lead, which extends beyond the end of the wooden part and comes to a point when sharpened.
- A bicycle is a machine for riding on. It consists of a metal frame and two rubber tyres.
- A computer is a machine with an enormous number of uses ranging from simple word processing to extremely complex data processing. It basically consists of a keyboard, a mouse, a screen and a disk-drive. It is made of metal and plastic.

3.8 You may need to prompt some students with ideas (see 2.8 above).

3.9 Monitor students carefully and help weak students to focus on suitable expressions and to practise the expressions.

3.10 Read 3.11 with the class so that they realise they must listen to each other to select one item from someone else's list to present to the whole class later.

Emphasise that each person has only five minutes to present their items. Make sure that each group has a time keeper to ensure this timing is kept to. The time keeper should warn speakers after four minutes that they have one minute left and stop them after five minutes.

3.11 Allow the students five minutes to make notes and check with the original presenter any points they are not sure of. Tell them to explain why they chose the item.

3.12 This can be done as a whole-class activity in small classes (ten or more students) or in sub-groups if the class is larger than ten.

Step 4: Language review [10m]

See page xv for a note on conducting this type of task.

Step 5: Before the next session

3.15 Refer students to the questionnaire on page 23 of Unit 3 in the Student's Book and tell them to complete the middle column before the next class.

LEARNER DIARY THREE

See page xvi for a detailed note on how to conduct this task.

UNIT 3

EDUCATION

You need to prepare: cassette player and cassette for Task 1.3.

SESSION 1

Step 1: Warm-up [5m]

1.1   Monitor and help weaker students with suitable adjectives.

1.2   Emphasise that the descriptions should not be detailed.

Step 2: Listening and note taking [20m]

1.3   Before playing the recording (6m 17s, tapescript on pages 89–91 of Student's Book), remind students of good note-taking[1] practice including the use of:

- symbols
- abbreviations
- headings
- numbering
- branching (ideas maps)/linear notes as appropriate.

Tell students in advance that they will hear the recording twice. Encourage students to compare answers with a partner after the first listening.

Step 3: Information transfer[25m]

It is important that *both* people have enough time to speak about their country here.

1.4   Go over the questions in the questionnaire on page 23 with students, dealing with any difficulties. Question 4 may need an explanation; it refers to a centrally controlled curriculum specified by the Ministry of Education in a country that all schools must follow. Tell the students to use their notes from 1.3 to complete as much as they can of Column A.

1.5   Ensure that students have enough time to complete this task; if they are from different countries, divide the time in two and insist they change over at the half-way point. If they are from the same country, make sure they discuss all the questions in the time available.

Questionnaire: Education in England		
	A) In England	B) In my country C) In another country
1. Between which ages is education compulsory?	5–16.	
2. Are schools free or fee-paying?	State schools are free; private/public schools are fee-paying.	
3. What are the stages and ages of pupils in the school system?	State schools: 5–11 primary; 11–18 secondary (16–18 sixth form).	
4. Do you have a national (i.e. centrally controlled) curriculum?	Yes.	
5. What qualifications can pupils get at school?	At 16: General Certificate of Secondary Education (GCSE) At 18: A-levels (Advanced level examination)	
6. How do pupils get into university?	They apply through a central admissions system in their final year at school and are made offers dependent on their A-level results.	
7. How long is the average undergraduate course?	Three years	

SESSION 2

 Step 1: Language focus [15m]

2.1   Before students look at the transcript try to elicit a range of signpost expressions, by asking questions such as: 'How can speakers signal to their audience how their talk will be structured?' or 'How can speakers show that they are moving on to a new topic?' Try to elicit some of the expressions that appear on the expression cards used in 2.3. These expressions, which are listed under 2.3, do not appear in the Student's Book.

A copy of the transcript of the talk is included in the Student's Book (pages 89-91).

2.2   Here is the transcript with the relevant parts in bold:

THE ENGLISH EDUCATION SYSTEM

The first point that should be made about the English education system is that it's seen enormous changes since the 1980s. This makes it very difficult to give a clear description of the system that we now have. Today I'm going to do my best to describe the system as I understand it. **I'm going to divide my talk into three broad sections: the first part** will be
5   looking at the school system itself; **the second part** will briefly look at tertiary level education in this country – universities; and **the third part** will consider some of the issues for the future, as I see it.

Right, **let's begin with** the school system. Schools in England **can be broadly divided into two categories**. **The first** is the state school system, which is free to all students, paid for by the
10 state. **The second category** is the independent or 'public' school system, which is fee-paying. **My focus** today is going to be on the first category, the state school system, which educates 93% of our pupils, so **we're looking here at** state schools **not** independent or 'public' schools.

So, the state school system. This **can broadly be divided into two types** of education: there's primary level education and secondary level education. Primary school begins at
15 the age of five in England. Children stay in primary school until the age of 11 and then they change to secondary school, where they must stay until the age of 16. Pupils can choose to leave school at 16 if they want to, or they can stay on at school to complete the final two years of education, which is called the sixth form.

Since 1988 we've had a national curriculum in our state schools, and this specifies **the**
20 **following main points**. **First of all**, there are three core subjects, and these are English, maths and science. All pupils are assessed in these subjects by national tests at certain stages in their education. There are eight other, foundation subjects: history, geography, design and technology and so on, which are not nationally assessed. The national curriculum covers state school studies up to the age of 16, when pupils take what are
25 called the GCSE examinations, that's the General Certificate of Secondary Education.

After the age of 16, pupils who stay on at school and choose to have an academic education, do two years in the sixth form and study for A-levels (that's advanced level examinations). These are taken in just three subjects, three or four subjects only – arts or sciences, usually – and these are the entrance requirements for university.
30 When students reach the age of 16, as I said, they can stay on at school and do A-levels if they want, or they can leave school and attend a college of further education, which will also provide A-level study or more vocational training too.

Students who get satisfactory A-level results can go on to university and **that's the second topic I want to look at today**. School pupils apply to universities through a central
35 admissions system in their final year of school. Universities either offer them a place which depends upon how they do in their A-levels (so they are told, 'You must get the following A-level results to get into our university') or they reject them, based upon their school's estimation of their ability and the competition from other pupils. There are 96

40 universities in the United Kingdom to choose from at the moment and the average full-time undergraduate course lasts three years for most academic subjects, four years for language courses and five for subjects such as medicine and veterinary science.

So let's now turn to the third thing I want to discuss: issues for the future. It's difficult to predict these as there seem to have been so many aspects of education over the last few years that have come to the public's attention. This is because of the dramatic

45 changes in the education system and the many conflicts that arose as a result, in the eighties and early nineties, between teachers and the government. So all this has led to lots of discussions about education standards and priorities, which I am sure will continue. **With reference to** standards, people will continue to be worried about core skills, particularly in primary school where basic levels of literacy and numeracy must be

50 established. **Regarding** priorities, another debate that won't go away, I suspect, is about the lack of emphasis our system puts on technical and vocational training as opposed to the more traditional academic education. More important to many parents and teachers will be the priority given to education in terms of funding; people will argue that more money should go into schools, **firstly**, to reduce class sizes and, **secondly**, to ensure that

55 classrooms are well equipped with the latest technology to ensure our school leavers have the skills needed by an increasingly sophisticated workplace. And **last**, but by no means least, attention will focus on how teachers are selected and trained, as without good teachers the best system will fail. These seem to me to be some of the main issues for the future, although I am sure others will also arise.

60 **I hope that this quick summary has been useful**, but **I would like to reiterate** my first point, that really our education system has gone through enormous changes in recent years. Education has become a very sensitive issue politically and I think it will be very interesting to see what direction it takes in the future.

Discuss with students other ways of helping the listeners when giving a talk. Elicit linguistic expressions which they can add to their list e.g. using an OHT with headings on it, providing a handout, pausing before a new section.

 ## Step 2: Short presentations [30m]

2.3 Copy each of the 'Useful expressions for discussion and presentation' in italics below onto individual cards to make a set of expression cards for each group of three or four students in your class. The boxed section on the following pages may be photocopied and the expressions in italics cut up for this purpose (without the headings).

Useful expressions for discussion and presentation

1. **Introducing the topic**

    The subject of this talk/presentation is …

    I'm going to talk about …

    My topic today is …

2. **Preliminaries**

    I'll be happy to answer any questions afterwards.

    If you have any questions, I'll do my best to answer them at the end.

    Perhaps I should clear up one point before I start: …

3. **Outlining the structure of the presentation in advance (= giving an overview)**

    I'm going to deal with three aspects of this subject: first I shall say something about … I shall then go on to say something about … Finally, I shall look at …

    What I have to say falls into three main sections: first, I'll talk about …

4. **Indicating the start of a new section**

    The next aspect I'd like to consider is …

    Moving on now to …

    Turning next to …

    I'd now like to turn to …

    That brings me to my next point …

    The second questions I'd like to discuss is …

5. **Referring to visual aids**

    As you can see in this chart, …

    This diagram shows that …

    If you look at this map, you'll see that …

    In this diagram, X represents …

    You can see from this chart that …

    It is clear from this graph that …

6. Concluding

So, to sum up …

In conclusion, I'd like to reiterate/emphasise that …

*So, to remind you of what I've covered in this talk, I started by **VB**ing …*

So, we've looked at …, and we've seen that …

Unfortunately, I seem to have run out of time. I shall therefore conclude very briefly by saying that …

7. Asking for clarification

I'm afraid I didn't follow your point about … Could you go over that again?

Could you go over what you said about …?

Could you explain what you meant when you said that …?

Could you give an example of what you had in mind when you said …?

Could you expand a little on what you said about …?

Could you be more specific about …?

8. Asking questions

I have a question about … : …?

9. Responding to a question

I'd prefer to deal with that point later.

I'm coming to that in a minute.

Yes, that's a good question …

10. Responding to an answer

Sorry. I'm still not quite clear about …

That's not really what I was asking. My question was about …

Perhaps my question wasn't clear. What I'd like to know is …

I see what you mean, but don't you think that …?

I see your point, but …

Explain the task to the students. Tell them that there are different categories of expressions according to their precise function. Tell them that they should decide, as a group, which expressions belong to the same category; you may wish to give an example to weaker students.

Monitor closely and give clear, evaluative feedback on what the groups produce, either to each group individually or to the class as a whole.

2.4 You may wish to simplify and speed up this task by eliciting from/giving students a list of labels/titles, one for each group of expressions. Suggested labels are in bold in the list of expressions above.

2.5 These are not the only ways of classifying these expressions; students may come up with other ways of doing it which could be equally valid.

2.6 'Speaker expressions': 1, 2, 3, 4, 5, 6, 9.

'Audience expressions': 7, 8, 10.

2.7 Prepare a set of topic cards suitable for your own class. You need at least four topics (i.e. one for each member of a group). With the more advanced classes you can maintain topical coherence across the unit by using education-related topics e.g. 'university education in my country', 'payment for education in my country', 'who controls education in my country?', 'the problems faced by my country's education system today'. With the less advanced classes you will need to use a range of broader topics, e.g. sport, television, food or holidays. Previous topics may be recycled.

2.8 Go through the notes in the example topic with the students and give (or get a good student to give) the talk based on the notes.

2.9 Tell the students to put all the cards into two piles: 'speaker expressions' and 'audience expressions', omitting the expressions under point 10. They should mix up each pile of cards and place them face downwards. All the students take their cards before the talk starts: the speaker takes three at random from the 'speaker expressions' pile and the listeners take one each at random from the 'audience expressions' pile. Demonstrate, if necessary. Stress to the listeners the importance of preparing a question so they have one ready at the end of the 90 seconds. Explain that it is important to keep strictly to time so that everyone can·have their turn at being the speaker.

2.10 Ensure an efficient changeover of speaker.

Step 3: Before the next session [5m]

2.11 It may be necessary to suggest sub-topics here, e.g.

a) level of education (primary, secondary, tertiary); class size; teacher training; vocational training; traditional ways of teaching and learning; state and private education;

b) dealing with technology in schools; ensuring school-leavers have the skills the country needs; paying for education.

Go through the information in the 'Remember the following' box to make sure everyone understands what they must do. Emphasise that one aim is to practise the use of signpost expressions to help the audience understand the organisation of a presentation.

Session 3

Step 1: Presentations [45m]

3.1   Explain the procedure to the students that during each presentation the listeners must take notes and, after each presentation, they will compare their notes with the speaker's notes.

3.2   Encourage efficient timing. As you go from group to group, monitor for speakers' use of signpost expressions, for feedback later.

3.3   Monitor for students' recognition of main points and quality of speakers' notes. If groups are answering 'no' to the questions here, encourage them to think of why this is so and what improvements could be made.

3.4   This can be done individually or in groups, followed by a class discussion. Answers that might be given include:

   a) by speaking more slowly, loudly and emphatically; by stating explicitly that this is the main point ('The main thing I want to say is …'); by making the point forcefully in the conclusion and also, perhaps, in the introduction;

   b) by giving an overview of how the argument will develop in the introduction (as in 2.3, number 3 above) and numbering points during the presentation; by pausing before each new point of the argument; by using language to indicate new sections (as in 2.3, number 4 above);

   c) by signalling it verbally (as in 2.3, number 6 above); by pausing to get the audience's attention, then speaking more slowly and emphatically.

   In all three cases, looking directly at the audience when saying these important parts of a presentation helps ensure the message is received and allows the speaker to see if people are following.

Step 2: Group discussion and mini-presentation [45m]

You may wish to keep students in the same groups as for Step 1 or re-group them.

3.5   Encourage group members to negotiate here, drawing ideas from the strengths and weaknesses of their own country's system, as well as from their own ideal conception. Weaker students may need more prompting with ideas. Students should not look at 'The ideal education' on page 27 until they have discussed the topic in their groups.

3.6   Students rank their choice in order of the most important features, with 1 as the most important, adding their own ideas from their group's discussion in 3.5 under 15-18 on page 27.

3.7 Here the students are being asked to decide on the main idea about education which will shape their mini-presentation in 3.9. Examples could be:

'We think the main purpose of education at school is to prepare responsible citizens who will benefit the country.'

'We think education at school should develop each individual's potential to the full.'

'We think children should be taught the skills they will need for future employment.'

'School should be fun so children want to learn.'

3.8 Tell students how much time each group will have for its mini-presentation. This will depend on the number of groups in the class, but a minimum would be five minutes per group.

Emphasise the need in an academic context to justify choices and opinions to other academics.

Language Help sections that could be useful here include: **Agreeing and disagreeing** (page 125), **Cause and effect** (page 128), **Describing trends** (page 132-134), **Expressing opinion** (page 135), **Expressing proportion** (page 136).

3.9 You may wish to give brief feedback on the mini-presentations and/or ask the class to decide on the most persuasive.

Step 3: Language review [10m]

See page xv for a note on conducting this type of task.

Step 4: Before the next session

3.12 Make sure the students understand this task.

---

1. See J. Trzeciak and S.E. Mackay (1994) *Study Skills for Academic Writing*, Prentice Hall, Unit 2 for guidance on note taking.

UNIT

4 *THE FAMILY*

You need to prepare: blank OHTs or poster sheets, and pens, for Task 2.4.

SESSION 1

Step 1: Discussion [20m]

1.1 The purpose of this activity is to have a lively discussion associated with the unit topic which will then be analysed by the group for the features affecting the success of the discussion.

You may like to choose a different topic related to the family. Topics need to be a bit controversial to promote discussion, e.g. 'Dependence on or independence from the family – which is better?', 'Children should be encouraged to be independent', 'It is not the responsibility of the family to look after "old people"'.

Appoint one person in each group as the observer, whom you brief while the others are noting down ideas to contribute to the discussion.

The observers will look at one basic aspect of group dynamics: to whom does each speaker in the group direct his comments? Give each observer a copy of Observation Sheet 1 on page 119 in the Student's Book. Ensure that they understand what to do before and during the discussion. An example of a completed observation sheet is included on page 36 of these notes for you to show the observers at this point. If there is a lot of communication, suggest that, instead of drawing a new arrow for each speaker's turn, the observer adds another arrow-head to an existing arrow for each turn (see the diagram below, where Aysha and Carlo address several comments to each other). If a speaker addresses the whole group, not one individual, suggest the observer shows this with an arrow from the speaker towards the centre of the box (as in Keiko's case).

1.2 Stress that the observers should not participate in the discussion.

OBSERVATION SHEET 1

INSTRUCTIONS FOR THE OBSERVER

Before the discussion: Write the name of one member of your group in each corner of the box below to represent the group's seating arrangements. Do not write your own name in the box.

During the discussion: Each time that someone speaks, draw one or more arrows to show the addresser (i.e. the person who spoke) and the addressee(s) (i.e. the person(s) to whom the addresser spoke).

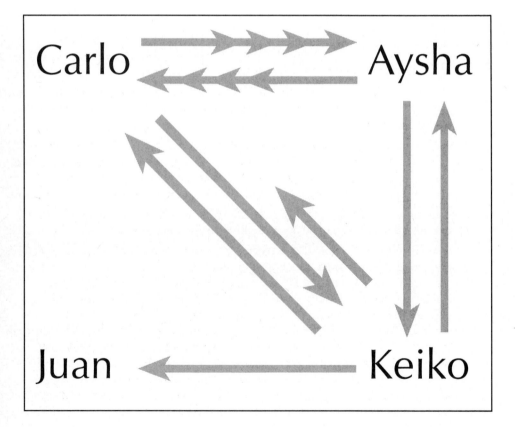

Step 2: Feedback on group dynamics [20m]

1.3   Ask the groups to consider why they answer 'yes' or 'no' here. Monitor groups carefully, making sure everyone is contributing. Some groups may not have 'managed' the discussion at all and you can encourage these groups to consider whether this was a problem and, if so, how they could have managed the discussion.

1.4   At this point the observer shows and explains what the completed diagram represents. Then the group interprets the diagram together. Looking at the example given here, points that arise are:

    a) • Carlo and Aysha speak to each other a lot more than they address others in the group

       • Juan does not speak at all

       • Keiko is the only person who speaks to everyone

       • Keiko is the only person who addresses a point to the group as a whole.

    b) • the group does not really have a group discussion as not everyone takes part

       • when people do speak, they mostly address other individuals in the group, not the group as a whole

       • discussion within the group is not balanced as some people address each other much more than they address others, so it almost becomes a private conversation.

1.5   Monitor carefully. 'Developing a shape or sense of direction' involves having a coherent discussion that flows well and reaches a conclusion of some kind (even if it is only 'we agree to differ on this topic').

1.6   Students work individually to complete the table. Remind them of the questions they considered for homework (Unit 3, 3.12) from **Reviewing Discussion: Checklist 3** on page 118 in the Student's Book ('Part 1 The Individual') when completing the 'My contribution' part of the diagram.

    A completed diagram could include the following:

My contribution	The group
1. Make sure I have at least two points to make on the topic before we start.	1. Appoint a chairperson who ensures everyone gets a chance to speak.
2. Ask people to explain if I don't understand their point.	2. Everyone tries to address their points to the whole group.
3. Check that people have understood me.	3. No 'private conversations' between individuals in the group.
4. Bring other people into the discussions by asking them a direct question.	4. Everyone agrees to wait for hesitant speakers to make their point, without interrupting.
5. Learn how to introduce a new topic.	5. Nobody monopolises the discussion for more than five minutes.

1.7 In plenary, elicit students' ideas. The basic points that this discussion should bring out are that successful group dynamics involve:

- everyone making some contribution
- no one person dominating at the expense of others' ability to contribute
- no one holding the floor for too long
- the speaker not always addressing the same one person
- the speaker responding to listeners' desire to come into the discussion.

Step 3: Collecting information on British families [10m]

1.8 This is a warm-up activity that will focus the students' attention on the topic to be read about and discussed. Make sure the students write down their points here as they will be needed next session (in 2.1).

1.9 Ask half of the class to look at Text A (Student's Book, pages 68-69) and the other half to look at Text B (pages 72-73). Students looking at the same text should be grouped together. Students tend to find Text A more difficult so this could be given to students of a higher level in the class.

1.10 The reading and highlighting of main points should be done as homework. Interpretation may vary, but a suggested highlighting of main points is given here on pages 39–42.

THE FAMILY IN BRITAIN
TEXT A
WITH MAIN POINTS HIGHLIGHTED

FACES OF THE FAMILY

Our desire to procreate, to parent, to carry on the family name, if a little depleted, remains strong. But which parent? Whose name? Having children has respectably broken beyond the confines of the marital bed. **Families have changed their shape, they've thrown up new norms and new dilemmas**. Beneath it all, have the foundations really been shaken?

TWO POINT TWO[1]

5   Tabloids[2] suggest that the family structure is disintegrating and the nuclear family has fragmented. In part that's true. The breadwinner dad and stay-at-home mum with two kids reflects the lifestyle of a tiny minority. **The most common family form – a married couple with dependent children – accounts for only 40 per cent of the population, although the mum-dad set-up still represents the family experience for the vast majority of**
10 **British youngsters.**
      What has really changed is that **no one kind of family dominates our society.** Families now come in many different guises. There have been **two startling trends over the last 20 years or so**. The first is the **huge increase in the number of children born to parents who are not married**. The second is the **substantial growth in the number of people living**
15 **alone.** A quarter of all households are made up of single people – twice as many as in 1961. And the fastest-growing group is single men under pension age.
      The **size of the family unit has also changed significantly**. This is partly **because of the growth in the number of people living alone and partly because people are having fewer children**. In fact, the number of young people has dropped considerably. In 1988 there
20 were 11.5 million under sixteens compared with well over 14 million at the beginning of the 1970s. Fewer couples than ever are producing large families. In the last 30 years, the percentage of households with five or more children has halved to just 8 per cent.
      Why is it that despite a one-third drop in infant mortality rates in the last ten years, there are fewer children? One factor has to be that **women are producing their babies**
25 **later. Wider career opportunities, economic independence and later marriage mean that many women, particularly those who are better educated, prefer to let motherhood wait**. The longer they leave it, the fewer fertile years they have in which to produce offspring. Some argue that current public and corporate attitudes towards parenting – expensive childcare and few genuine family-friendly policies – along with the inevitable penalties for
30 a break in a career, have made women reluctant to relinquish their hard-won places on the career ladder.
      Perhaps also, **children hold less significance in women's lives**. A survey by the National Council of Women showed that only 13 per cent of all women of child-bearing age, and one quarter of mothers, agree that a woman needs a child in order to feel fulfilled.

THREE SCORE AND TEN[3]

35 It's not just birth rates that set the pattern of family relationships but also **the average life-span**. There are currently well over ten and a half million pensioners in Britain. By the second decade of the next century almost a fifth of the population will be aged over 65. That's twice as many older people as in 1950. This tipping of the population scales has far-reaching consequences for the community.

40   At the turn of the century a woman reaching her sixtieth birthday could expect to live for a further 14 or so years; a man, another 13. Today, that same couple could look forward to a further 22 and 18 years respectively. **What is critical is the number of men and women living to a very ripe old age**. In 1901 there were just 57,000 people aged over 85. A hundred years later that number is expected to top one million.

45   Older people are not a homogeneous group and the picture is very different for men and women. The vast majority of older men are married – even a sizeable proportion of the over-85s. By contrast, only a minority of women are still married over 65. Overall, **most older people are living with their spouse. However, the majority of women over 80 live alone**. And to prove the extended family is alive and kicking, **a sizeable number live**
50 **with relatives**.

      Older people don't just have greater life expectancy than their forebears, they are also **fitter and active for more years**. A recent survey showed that pensioners have never felt better, many saying they were more satisfied with their life now than in their youth. Clearly older people – a fifth of the population – are not about just to take to the rocking chair.

55   As people continue to live longer, so **the number of three- and four-generation families will increase**. This will inevitably have an impact on the interaction within the new extended family unit. **An ageing population also raises the crucial question about care. If the state can't or won't cope, will the family?**

      From T. Aleksander, *Faces from the family*, Channel 4 Television, 1994.

1. Two point two: this refers to the figure (2.2) often quoted for the average number of children per family in Britain.

2. Tabloids: popular newspapers which tend to sensationalise stories.

3. Three score and ten: this antiquated form refers to the number of years (70) traditionally considered a full life-span.

THE FAMILY IN BRITAIN
TEXT B
WITH MAIN POINTS HIGHLIGHTED

BRITISH FAMILY LIFE IN THE 1990's

What is clear about Britain in the 1990s is that it is **more socially acceptable to have alternative life styles, relationships and ways of bringing up children** than it has ever been. It is also easier to remove oneself from an unhappy family situation. In most social groups, **divorce is no longer seen as taboo**.[1] One-parent families are common. **Many children are**
5   **given more freedom when young**; when they move away from home, they move earlier (usually at around 18), and go further. People experiment with relationships before committing themselves to marriage and there is greater acceptance of homosexual relationships. **In Britain's multi-cultural society there are many examples of different ways of living**. Nowadays, our primary sexual characteristics – whether we are men or women –
10 no longer seem to completely dictate what roles we should take in life.

WORKING MOTHERS

Until relatively recently, most mothers in Britain did not take paid work outside the home. Sometimes women did voluntary work, especially those of the middle classes. However, most women's main (unpaid) labour was to run the home and look after their family. Whether they did this themselves or supervised other people doing it was a matter
15 of class and money. **By entering the labour market, women have now altered the face of family life**. As the role of the woman in the family changed, so did the role of the man.

EQUALITY IN WORK?

Recent legal changes have given women new opportunities. In 1970, the Equal Pay Act attempted to stop discrimination against women in the field of employment. In 1975 the Sex Discrimination Act was a further attempt to protect women in employment,
20 education and other areas. The 1975 Employment Protection Act gave women the right to maternity leave.

In Britain today **women make up 44 per cent of the workforce**, and nearly half the mothers with children under five years old are in paid work. It is not uncommon to find that the mother is the main breadwinner.[2] The incentives for women to work or to
25 return to work are increasing all the time, but **there are still problems for women who want or have to work**.

Although there is a greater acceptance of men taking more of an interest in childcare and domestic duties, studies show that **men's and women's roles have not changed as much as could be expected**. In most families working women are still mothers, housekeepers
30 and income providers. There is a stigma[3] attached to the phenomenon of 'latch key kids'.[4] Society expects someone – usually the mother – to be there. **Because of the difficulties of combining the mother role with the demands of a career, women's work also tends to be low-paid and irregular**.

CHILDCARE

Britain is old-fashioned as regards maternity leave.[5] If they do get maternity leave, women
35 are often worried that, if they do not return to work quickly, they will lose their job and it
is often very difficult for them to find another. Paternity leave – time off for the father –
is rare, although it is becoming common in other European countries.

A big problem for working mothers in the UK is **the low standard of childcare
facilities for pre-school children**. Parents may employ a nanny[6] to come to their home or
40 to live with them. This is very expensive and only realistic for a small percentage of
families. An alternative is childcare centres run by the local council, where a child-
minder[7] looks after children during the day in the minder's own home. It is not always
easy to get a place in one of these centres.

**Once their children have reached school age, most women in Britain work part-time,
45 to fit in with school hours.** However, this is not always possible for women who want a
career. Recently there has been **increasing pressure on the Government to provide more
money for state day nurseries, and on employers to establish crèches[8] in the workplace**.

From C. Addis, *Britain Now, Book One*, BBC English 1992 pp. 29–31

1. taboo: socially unacceptable because it is considered offensive or embarrassing.
2. breadwinner: person supporting a family financially by earning money.
3. stigma: a reputation of shame or dishonour.
4. latch key kids: children who have their own key to their home because there is no one to let them in after school.
5. maternity leave: paid time off for a woman who is having or caring for a baby.
6. nanny: child nurse trained to a high standard.
7. child-minder: a person who is qualified to look after children.
8. crèches: nurseries.

SESSION 2

Step 1: Preparing for a presentation [40m]

2.1   If you have a small class, the students can easily split into two groups of up to five people according to which text they read. If the class has more than ten people, you should divide them into groups of four or five according to the text read. During the presentations in Session 3, only one person will present each text, so you will have to select from several presenters at that stage.

Ask students to put a tick next to points they were right about, a cross next to those they were wrong about and a question mark next to things they are still unsure of.

2.2   This is a group activity. You may want to prompt the groups as to what would be suitable headings. Suggest they look at the sub-titles in the texts and see how useful they are.

Suggested headings for Text A:

1) The changing shape of British families

2) The size of families

3) The increase in the average life-span

4) The effects of an ageing population

Suggested headings for Text B:

1) Recent trends in British family life

2) Working mothers

3) Childcare

2.3   Another group activity. Emphasise the importance of writing clear, concise notes under each heading.

2.4   Another group activity. Recap points of writing good OHTs/posters (see notes on Unit 1, 2.3 on pages 12 and 13).

2.5   Do not allow the weakest students to present on behalf of the group. The chosen presenters should practise here, with emphasis on a clear, informative presentation keeping within the time limit.

Step 2: Before the next session [10m]

Make sure everyone understands that they must prepare and rehearse their presentation and come fully prepared, with notes, to the next session.

2.6   If your class size is large and several groups have worked on presenting both texts, you must now select one presenter for Text A and one presenter for Text B to present at the next session. The other groups' presenters must join the rest of the class in doing Task 2.7.

Make sure that presenters of Texts A and B are clear about what they have to do for the next session.

2.7 See 3.11 in the Student's Book. Go over what they have to do with the class members who are not preparing a presentation on either text.

For students from the same country, select a range of topics relevant to discussion of the family in that country. Give each topic to several people (depending on how many groups you will have in 3.10). Topics might include:

- the typical family of the past
- the typical family of today
- the typical family of the future
- the role of women within the family
- the role of men within the family
- the role of grandparents within the family
- the generation gap within families
- issues facing the family today
- rural and urban families.

SESSION 3

Your role as time keeper will be very important in this session. If presenters are allowed to overrun the time limit excessively, interest is likely to decrease and there will not be time for everyone to contribute.

Step 1: Presentation [5m]

3.1 During the presentation of Text A:

- Those who read that text should have their notes on the text in front of them to check the accuracy of what is said and they should note down any discrepancies.
- Those who read the other text take notes so that they can identify points that are unclear to ask question about in 3.3.

Step 2: Following the presentation [20m]

3.2 Remind the class that corrections to content only are required at this point. Invite corrections gently – by commenting on the strengths of the presentation and asking the presenter to make any comments or self-corrections first. Ask the same text readers to correct constructively and positively. (Refer to **Agreeing and disagreeing**, page 125, and **Referring to a text**, page 138, in the Language Help section.) Any suggested corrections can be checked against the text.

3.3 Allow the presenter to answer the questions from the other text's readers. If he cannot answer, allow the other Text A readers to respond.

3.4 You should either provide photocopies of **Assessing Presentations: Checklist for Unit 4** (on page 32 of the Student's Book) for students to complete, or ask students to make clearly numbered responses on a blank sheet of paper as follows:

1. Quite
2.a) yes
  b) no
  c) no
3. Yes
4.a) about right
  b) too quiet
  c) expressive
5.a) some
  b) some
6.a) most
  b) most
7. Speak louder. Use larger writing on the poster – all difficult words and figures should be on the poster. Keep to time so you don't have to rush at the end.

While students are completing their checklists here, the teacher should give the presenter feedback on language points.

Step 3: Second presentation [20m]

3.5   Repeat Steps 1 and 2 above for the Text B presentation.

Step 4: Feedback [15m]

This part of the class needs sensitive handling. As far as possible, focus on the strengths of the presentations, allowing the presenters to point out areas of improvement themselves.

3.6   Students give completed checklists to presenters.

3.7   The presenters should now read through the checklists and note improvements they could make in the next presentation. Tell the rest of the class to decide on two or three strengths of the presentations.

3.8   The groups summarise the strengths of the presentations.

3.9   You may prefer to place students in groups for this activity.

Step 5: Presentations [40m]

3.10   The intention here is to redivide the group so that students are working with some different people from those they worked with on Text A or B. If your class is larger than ten students, you will need to have more than two groups, with a maximum of five people per group.

With a *mixed-nationality* class, if there are students from the same country, try to make sure they are in different groups.

For classes with students from the *same* country, make sure that each group is composed of students with different topics, as assigned in 2.7.

3.11 Make sure the class realises the importance of the timekeeper's role here.

3.12 Groups should spend five minutes advising the chosen person on improvements to the presentation.

3.13 Only two or three of the people chosen in 3.12 will be able to give their presentations to the whole class here. If the class consists of a larger number of groups, select people who performed well in their group presentation.

With weak classes, suggest they write down their question(s).

3.14 Monitor who asks questions to ensure a few individuals are not dominating.

Step 6: Language review [homework]

See page xv for a note on conducting this type of task.

UNIT 5

THE MEDIA

SKILLS FOCUS: Giving an overview

You need to prepare: (optional) copy of *Radio Times* or other TV listings for Task 1.2;
cassette(s) and cassette player(s) for Task 2.4.

SESSION 1

Step 1: Warm-up [5m]

1.1 You may want to lead into this task, and the unit in general, by first eliciting very quickly a working definition of 'the media' and some examples.

The purpose of this task is to introduce the topic of the media. The vocabulary items given here, and some of the ideas that come up when the students explain their selections, are likely to be recycled in the presentation and discussion tasks in Session 3. You can make the activity livelier and more engaging by copying the list onto the board beforehand, so that students do not have to look down at their books. If you think that a longer or shorter, higher- or lower-tech list than the one given in the Student's Book would be better for your class, modify it accordingly.

Step 2: Vocabulary – different kinds of programme [12m]

If possible, take with you into class at least one copy of the current *Radio Times* (or some other TV listings in English) for these tasks. It will serve as an easy way of introducing the subject of different kinds of programme, and as a source of current examples of the various kinds of programme.

The purpose of the task is to familiarise students with some of the vocabulary which will be used in the listening task in Session 2, and which will be useful to students outside class for discussion of their viewing preferences – a common topic of conversation on the campus as elsewhere.

1.2 Matching definitions [5m]

KEY

soap opera	4	sitcom	1
quiz show	8	documentary	2
game show	7	classic drama	3
chat show	6	phone-in	5

1.3 Discussion [7m]

Divide the class into groups of two or three students for this discussion. Monitor to check that the vocabulary items from 1.2 are being used correctly.

If you are teaching a class of international students near the beginning of their stay in an English-speaking country, they would probably be very interested to receive some personal viewing tips from their teacher.

 ## Step 3: Describing charts [36m = 10m + 8m + 5m + 5m]

The main purpose of these tasks is to give students further practice at describing charts. Because charts can make complex information look deceptively simple, it sometimes comes as a surprise to students and teachers alike to find how difficult they can be to describe in a foreign language. Complex language structures may be necessary to convey the complex information precisely. These tasks therefore include controlled practice of some expressions for specifying precisely what the subject matter of the chart is.

1.4 Transferring information from a chart [10m]

Instruct half of the class to look at Chart 1 on page 67 of the Student's Book, and the other half at Chart 2 on page 75. When they have had a minute or so to look at their chart individually, pair them with someone who has the same chart, to discuss the questions.

Explain that the programme categories in these charts are those used by the BBC for internal reporting, and that therefore they do not correspond exactly to the kinds of programme in 1.2. You can elicit/suggest certain likely points of correspondence: Which kinds of programme from 1.2 would be included, for example, under Entertainment? (sitcoms, quiz shows, game shows, …?); Which category would soap operas fall into? (drama, entertainment or daytime?).

1.5 Exchanging information [8m]

Emphasise the instruction in the Student's Book that, when answering questions in this exercise, students should refer to the chart rather than reading from their notes. This is to make the practice more communicative, less mechanical. For the same reason, although the same ten questions appear below both charts, the order of the questions differs in the two cases.

KEY

Chart 1

1. Which two categories of programme take up between them over half of the total hours produced? **News & Current Affairs and Sport**

2. Which is the third largest category as far as hours produced are concerned? **Factual**

3. Which is the smallest category in terms of programme hours produced? **Education**

4. Which three categories of programme account between them for only 12% of the total hours produced? **Education, Drama and Music & Arts**

Chart 2

1. Which is the largest category in terms of BBC production costs? **Drama**

2. Which are the three next largest categories as far as cost is concerned? **Factual, Entertainment and News & Current Affairs**

3. Which three categories of programme account between them for only 13% of the total production costs? **Daytime, Education and Music & Arts**

4. Which is the fourth smallest category in terms of cost? **Children's**

1.6   **Language practice** [8m]

Go through the example with the class, modelling the pronunciation including the rhythm. Ask which words in the complete statement are stressed; elicit an answer along the lines of 'the important information-bearing words'. The unmarked pattern would be: S̲p̲o̲r̲t̲ is the s̲m̲a̲l̲l̲est category in terms of c̲o̲s̲t̲.

Make sure students appreciate that the focus of this exercise is on structure and pronunciation, and that it is therefore not a model of communicative appropriacy. In natural communication the response to these questions would probably be in the form of a 'short answer' rather than a complete statement.

1.7   **Discussion** [5m]

This task provides some less controlled practice of the expressions focused on in the previous task. Allow students just two or three minutes to try to work out questions 1 and 2, then refer them to Chart 3 (Student's Book page 79) to check their answers before going on to discuss question 3.

KEY

1) Drama

2) Daytime (closely followed by Sport and News & Current Affairs)

1.8   **Consolidation** [5m]

This is suitable for setting as homework if classroom time runs out.

KEY

1 Drama
2 twice
3 Daytime
4 News & Current Affairs

SESSION 2

The central task in this session is a jigsaw listening. See page xiv for a note on how to conduct this type of task.

Step 1: Anticipation questions [10m]

2.1 You need to be familiar in advance with the content of the two listening texts (Student's Book pages 91–96), so that you can guide students appropriately in their selection of questions.

2.3 Elicit, and build up on the board, a list of questions of which:

a) the majority are answered, or at least touched on, in the listening texts;

b) some relate to the content of Text 1, and others to that of Text 2.

Step 2: Listening [25m]

2.4 Explain the procedure to the students. Give them the following information:

- how long the text lasts
- how much time they will have for listening and then comparing notes
- how long they will have (in Task 2.6) to tell someone else the main points.

Make sure the cassette is positioned at the beginning of the appropriate text, set the counter to zero, and give control of the cassette player to the students.

Step 3: Preparation – giving an overview [5m]

2.5 The main purpose of Tasks 2.5 and 2.6 is for students to practise using an overview to outline in advance for their listeners the structure of what they are going to say. (It builds on the elementary practice in Unit 3, Session 2.) Make sure that your students understand what is meant here by 'overview'.

Monitor and feedback by the teacher are particularly important here: before students proceed to 2.6, check to ensure that they are on the right lines with their headings, because the value of the next exercise will be much reduced if the headings they use are completely inappropriate.

Encourage students to rehearse their overview orally. A possible example of an overview based on the headings for Text 1 below might run as follows (the brackets contain optional material, which can be included to make the overview more specific):

> 'The speaker in Text 1 talked about three main areas: the funding of the BBC (how much it receives, and where it comes from), the question of the BBC's independence (is it really independent? the importance of the Charter in this connection), and, thirdly, changes at the BBC in recent years (in two main areas: programme budgets and technology).

There is some scope for variation in the headings used to organise a summary of the texts. The briefest possible set of headings is probably the following:

Text 1

The BBC

1) Funding

2) Independence (and the Charter)

3) Recent changes

Text 2

The BBC

1) Its public service role

2) Violence on TV (and in society)

Step 4: Exchanging information [10m]

2.6 Remind students how long they have for this task: four minutes each to summarise and one minute to deal with queries. After five minutes, tell them it is time to switch roles.

Circulate and monitor how effectively they manage to give their overviews.

Step 5: Review [8m]

2.7 See page xv for a note on the rationale of this type of task. When students have discussed the questions in pairs, move to a plenary round-up.

2.8 You can do this very quickly, if necessary, by going down the list on the board, and eliciting whether you should write T1 (= answered in Text 1), T2 (= answered in Text 2), or N (= not answered in either text) beside each question.

Step 6: Before the next session [30m homework]

2.9 Because this presentation task is intended to practise giving an overview, some teachers prefer not to allow the use of visual aids at the beginning of the presentation (i.e. no display outline of the kind practised in Unit 1). This obliges students to concentrate on making their spoken overview effective. If you want to follow this practice, inform your students at this point, before they start preparing the presentation.

If your students are all from the same country, instead of talking about 'the media in my country' at 3.3, each student could talk about one of the mass media (radio, or TV, or the press), or about the media in his country at a particular date (e.g. 1800, or 1900, or 2000).

Session 3

Step 1: Presentation [32m = (6m + 2m) × 4]

3.1   Divide the class into groups of three or four students, as diverse as possible in terms of country (or district) of origin. Allow a short time (say two minutes) for questions after each presentation.

Step 2: Review [5m]

3.2   The purpose here is for students to consider

a) how helpful an overview can be and

b) how else the presenter can help the listener to follow the presentation.

After students have carried out the review in their groups, round up their ideas quickly with the whole class.

Step 3: Preparation [5m]

3.3   To lead into this task, it is helpful to have available in class some recent newspaper articles concerned in some way with the power of the media. Show the headlines to the class and ask students if they know/can guess any of the details of the corresponding news stories. Discuss briefly the issues that arise.

When students are preparing for the discussion, monitor to ensure that they all note down at least two points as instructed in the Student's Book. If some of your students seem to find this very difficult, you may encourage them by telling them that the ideas they note down do not necessarily have to reflect their own personal views (although the discussion will probably be better if they do) – they can put forward an exaggerated version of their views if necessary.

Step 4: Language focus [5m]

3.4   Ask students if they can think of expressions that can be used to ask for clarification. Elicit as far as possible, then refer students to page 126 in the Language Help section and go through the expressions with the class, modelling pronunciation, including stress and intonation.

Step 5: Discussion and reporting back [25m]

3.5 Tell students that they have two objectives in this discussion: for each individual to contribute his ideas to the discussion, and for the group to reach some conclusion on the topic (i.e. that the media are on the whole a force either for good or for bad). Set a time limit for the discussion – 15 minutes is probably about right, depending on the level of your class. When half of the time has elapsed, tell students how long there is left for them to make their contributions to the discussion.

3.6 If you want a more extensive review activity at this stage, there is the option of using **Reviewing Discussion Checklist 3** (page 118 of the Student's Book).

Step 6: Language review [10m]

See page xv for a note on conducting this type of task.

UNIT 6 HEALTH

SKILLS FOCUS: Preparing a group presentation

You need to prepare: blank OHTs or poster-sheets and pens for task 1.2; optional: photocopies of Health questionnaires A and B on pages 41-42 of the Student's Book for Task 1.3.

SESSION 1

Step 1: Extending vocabulary [15m]

1.1 Students should work very quickly.

1.2 Place students in suitable groupings. Remind them of the logical groupings of words on a mind map. Ask one or two groups to present their mind maps to the class, explaining the logic of their organisation. Suggest other students add any new words to their maps.

Step 2: Collecting information [30m]

1.3 You may photocopy the Health questionnaire sheets for students to fill in or ask them to note down their answers on two sheets of paper clearly labelled A and B. If you have a class with more than twelve students, you must ensure they complete enough copies of the questionnaires for all groups to have a set of either A or B questionnaires from the whole class (see 1.4 below).

Check students' understanding of difficult items on the questionnaire in order to prevent time-consuming confusion later on.

Explain the overall task for this unit (i.e. collection, processing and interpretation of data, culminating in a presentation of findings by each group).

Advanced-level groups could be encouraged to add their own questions – or even design their own questionnaire on the topic. These questions reflect British people's current concerns on health and may be of less interest to students studying in a very different cultural environment.

1.4   The text in the Student's Book assumes the class can be divided into two groups for this activity. The maximum size for a group is six people, so if your class is larger than twelve, you will need to have more than one A and one B group. Divide the class into an even number of groups, with a maximum of six students per group, to process the data. Make sure there is an equal number of A and B groups.

1.5   Outline the stages of this activity with the class so that they understand what they have to do next session. Ask the students to begin work on 1) and 2) in their groups, and to note down any good suggestions, but explain that 3) will be done in the next session.

Strong classes can be left to negotiate, in English, by themselves how to do these tasks and this will be a useful speaking activity.

Weaker classes may need some guidance, as outlined below.

1) 'deciding on a procedure for processing the data' might include:

- allocating specific questionnaire questions to specific pairs of students
- deciding how to collate the data (e.g. raw scores or percentages?)
- setting deadlines.

2) 'processing the data' (in pairs) might include:

- counting the answers to your part of the questionnaire
- converting the answers to percentages if required
- presenting the results in a diagrammatic form (e.g. pie/bar charts) on a handout
- interpreting the data – looking for interesting patterns/findings
- preparing a talk on the data to give to others in the group who have not seen it yet, checking on any language problems with the teacher/other students.

For homework: Students could make sure their data has been processed as outlined above, so that next session they are ready to discuss their findings as a group.

SESSION 2

Step 1: Language focus [10m]

2.1   Discuss language useful for expressing proportion.

Step 2: Processing questionnaire data (15m]

2.2   For 1) here, elicit some questions from the whole class, to aid students in their discussion. They might include:

- What patterns are there in the class responses?
- Of what group (if any) is the class a typical sample?
- Which results are most likely to be of interest to the class?

- What interpretation, if any, can be made of these results?
- How confidently/tentatively should these interpretations be made?

The students then discuss the elicited questions in their groups and each pair of students could present their information to the whole group – as a short talk and a handout (if completed for homework as suggested above).

For 2) here, each group needs to decide how best to present their information. Issues may include:

- There will probably be variation in the ways different people have presented their data (e.g. as pie charts/bar charts or raw scores): do they want to keep this variation or standardise?
- Will everyone speak in the presentation?
- What language will they need?

Step 3: Preparing the group presentation [35m]

2.3 Emphasise the limited time here and the requirement for a group presentation involving at least three people – thus the need for group rehearsal and smooth transitions from one speaker to the next. Group members not speaking can prepare and present visuals (before and during the presentation).

Step 4: Before the next session

2.4 Emphasise that this is essential if the rehearsal in class has revealed problems/room for improvement.

SESSION 3

Step 1: Presentation of questionnaire results [35m]

3.1 Again time keeping needs to be strict.

If the class has more than one A and B group, either:

- choose one A and one B only to present to the whole class

  or

- split the whole class into sub-groups with an A and a B group in each for presentations

  or

- allow several presentations of A and B findings (gaining time by omitting Step 3 below).

3.2 Remind listeners to note down any queries they may have. Allow about five minutes of questions after each presentation. Anyone in the group may answer questions, not just the presenters.

Step 2: Feedback [10m]

3.3 The aim here is for the problems with the presentation to be pointed out by the presenters themselves, to develop their critical self-assessment skills, and for the listeners to focus on the presentation's strengths, preferably in comparison with their own presentation.

3.4 The groups take it in turns to present their feedback.

3.5 This should be done individually, then discussed as a whole class. This is an opportunity to discuss and stress the role of rehearsal for **any** presentation, and of feedback from an audience for a rehearsal.

Step 3: Discussion [55m]

This activity as outlined here takes the form of a formal debate. You could, however, choose to have a more informal discussion on the topic, with group discussion followed by presentations and whole class discussion. Whatever the format, the students will need to work quickly to assemble ideas and produce a convincing argument in the time available and this element of time pressure is important here.

3.6 Students should be regrouped here to provide variety. It would be sensible to place smokers in Group 2, but some students will probably have to argue against their genuine views.

Make sure the students all understand the procedure for the discussion/debate (see 3.10–3.12) and how much time they have before the debate/discussion begins. Specify that each speaker will have five minutes.

3.7 Encourage students to consider the points listed here, but stress that they do not have to include all or any of them if they have other ideas. Remind each group to select a secretary to note down the points raised.

Anticipating audience reaction and trying to prepare arguments to deal with it is an important presentation preparation skill.

3.8 Ideally, each spokesperson should have a number of points to raise that are connected in some way. The whole group should work on deciding the themes, and points for each speaker.

There is no time for rehearsal on this occasion.

3.9 Review the task of a chairperson:
- to introduce the topic very briefly
- to call upon the speakers to begin
- to make sure that each speaker keeps to the time limit of five minutes
- to make sure people in the audience get a fair chance to speak/ask questions after the speakers have all spoken
- to organise the voting at the end.

It is **not** the chairperson's role to give his/her opinions or to speak at length.

3.10   The spokespeople put forward their points of view. The following is the procedure for a traditional debate:

    1) Speaker 1 in favour of the topic

    2) Speaker 1 against the topic

    3) Speaker 2 in favour of the topic

    4) Speaker 2 against the topic.

    Speakers after 1) can refer to what previous speakers have said.

    Members of the audience should note down comments/questions for later.

3.11   It is the chairperson's job to throw the discussion open at this point. People who want to comment/ask a question should raise their hand and the chairperson must make sure as many people as possible get a chance to make their point in the time available.

3.12   In a traditional debate, the first speaker against the topic, then the first speaker in favour of it summarise their main arguments at this point. However, there will probably only be time for a whole class vote (by raising hands).

3.13   Not all the questions here will apply to everyone. The main speakers should be able to answer most of the questions; the members of the audience might look at Part 2 – but make sure this does not become a criticism of the chairperson.

 Step 4: Language review [10m]

See page xv for a note on conducting this type of task.

POPULATION AND MIGRATION

SKILLS FOCUS: Responding to questions

You need to prepare: cassette player and cassette for Task 1.1; blank OHTs or poster
sheets, and pens, for Task 3.2.

SESSION 1

Step 1: Listening [5m]

1.1 The listening text in this task presents an extract from a presentation, in which the
speaker describes trends with reference to a graph displayed as a visual aid. To
prepare students for the listening task, refer them to the graph in the book and
elicit:

   1) some basic graph-related lexis: *x axis, y axis, horizontal and vertical axes, curve,
   key, dotted line, broken line*;

   2) what the graph is about, what is missing from it, and which curve students
   think represents which country.

Tell students that, as in most real-life situations, they will hear the text once only.

KEY

Japan
Germany
UK
France

Step 2: Language focus [15m = 5m + 10m]

These two tasks focus more closely on the language forms for describing trends.

1.2 Before directing students to the tapescript (page 96), tell them to think back to the
listening text and ask if they can remember from it any language that is
particularly useful for describing trends.

Direct students to the tapescript (page 96). Allow them a few minutes working individually or in pairs, to look through the tapescript and underline the expressions that are particularly useful for describing trends. Monitor as they do so, to check, that they are on the right lines. Finally, quickly establish with the whole class which are the relevant expressions (see key below).

KEY

Unemployment in OECD Countries 1980–1992

This graph shows the changing levels of unemployment over the period 1980 to 1992 in four OECD countries: France, Germany, Japan and the UK. Of the four, Japan had the lowest level; unemployment remained fairly stable there, at between 2 per cent and 3 per cent throughout this period.

As you can see, this contrasted quite sharply with the UK. Unemployment here was relatively high and fluctuated considerably. It rose steeply from 6 per cent in 1980 to a peak of just over 12 per cent in 1983. It fell back in the late '80s, but then increased strongly again in the last two or three years of the period.

As in the UK case, Germany's unemployment peaked in 1983, though at the lower level of 7.5 per cent. However, the subsequent fall, to 6 per cent in 1988 and 4.5 per cent in 1992, was steadier and longer-lived.

In France, unemployment peaked comparatively late, in 1986–7. After a slight fall it was once again on an upward trend, after 1990.

1.3 The Language Help section contains more controlled practice of the language for describing trends than of the other functional areas. The reason for this is that during trialling teachers and students alike expressed the view that this functional area was of particular importance in EAP. However, students will vary in their need of controlled practice: more advanced classes will be able to run through the exercise orally without needing to prepare; less advanced classes may benefit from doing the exercise individually in writing first, before going through the answers orally. In either case, monitor to make sure that your students can use the lexis and structures confidently and correctly.

KEY (to **Describing trends** exercise on page 132 in Language Help section)

1. There was a **slight rise** in production between 1950 and 1960.
2. Production **rose slightly** between 1950 and 1960.
3. Consumption **fell sharply** between 1960 and 1980.
4. There was a **sharp fall** in consumption between 1960 and 1980.
5. Inflation **increased dramatically** after 1960, **peaking** at **16%** in 1970. It **has fallen steadily** since then.
6. **Production rose steadily after 1950, peaking at 310 litres in 1970. It then fell back sharply, to 160 litres in 1980 and just 130 litres in 1990. The decline now seems to have halted, and production is expected to rise steadily over the next decade.**

Step 3: Communication practice [25m = 5m + 8m + 12m]

1.4   Prediction [5m]

These questions anticipate the content of the two graphs used in the next activity. Elicit a working definition of *migration* (the word occurs in question 2), but do not labour the point as the reading text in Task 2.1 offers a definition.

1.5   Preparation [8m]

This preparation can be done either by individuals or, in the case of less advanced classes, by pairs of students who are looking at the same graph. Tell half of the class to look at page 66 (*World population growth since 1900*) and the other half at page 63 (*Legal immigrants admitted to the US: 1900–88*).

1.6   Exchanging information [12m]

See page xiv for a note on this type of task.

Step 4: Discussion [10m]

1.7   This task provides the opportunity for freer, more authentic practice of some of the language for describing trends. Go over the example in the Student's Book with the class.

1.8   This task anticipates the content of the reading texts that will be introduced in Session 2.

SESSION 2

Step 1: Reading [15m = 10m + 5m]

2.1   Before students see the texts, prepare them for the reading task by reminding them of their discussion in Task 1.8. Elicit from them two or three cases of migration and then some suggestions as to the factors involved.

Go through the form of the worksheet with the class, drawing students' attention to the point made in the Student's Book that each text will enable them to complete only half of the worksheet (Text A the first half of the worksheet, and Text B the second half). Direct half of the class to page 70 (*Mass migration in the modern era* - Text A) and the other half to page 78 (*Mass migration in the modern era* - Text B). Students work individually at this stage. Monitor to pick up on any major difficulties students may have in completing the relevant parts of the worksheet.

At the reading and note-taking stage, you can *either* tell students to take notes directly onto the worksheet in answer to the questions, *or* tell them first to take notes from the article onto a separate sheet and then to complete the worksheet by referring back to their notes. The latter option is probably more appropriate for classes whose reading and note-taking skills are relatively weak.

If necessary, remind your students to follow good note-taking practice here, e.g.

- be selective
- edit out incidental detail
- make use of symbols and abbreviations
- paraphrase as much as possible (don't simply copy chunks direct from the text).

Following this practice will enable them to explain their notes more easily and effectively in the subsequent information exchange.

The precise form of notes acceptable to you will depend on the level of your students and the note-taking techniques you have practised with them. One acceptable completion is illustrated on page 63.

2.2 Pair each student up with another who read the same text. Remind students that this task, like the next one (2.3), is an opportunity for them to practise oral explanation of ideas extracted from a written, academic text. It should therefore be done by speaking and listening only, not by students showing their notes to each other.

Monitor students (particularly those who are less advanced readers) to ensure that they have extracted the appropriate information, otherwise the value of the next task (2.3) is much diminished.

 Step 2: Exchanging information [10m]

2.3 Pair each student up with a partner who read the other text. When they have had sufficient time to exchange information, quickly run through the correct completion of the worksheet.

Worksheet: Mass migration in the modern era

1. Definition of migration:

Usual def. = (semi-) permanent change of residence
Here, between nations.

2. Factors influencing the decision to migrate:

Factor	Definition/example
push	From place of origin: e.g. no job opportunities religious persecution war famine
pull	To place of destination: usually economic (e.g. better jobs or land), but sometimes non-economic considerations (e.g. presence of relatives or compatriots) prevail.

intervening obstacles	= deterrents to migration:
	may outweigh strong push and pull factors:
	e.g. distance
	    trouble
	    cost
	    immigration procedure
	    likely problems on arrival

personal	e.g. life-stage (married? children?)
	    ability
	    personality

3. Consequences of migration:

Large numbers ➔ friction.

Receiving countries have experienced adjustment problems with each wave.

Newest arrivals usually get lowest-paid jobs. Face resentment from native population, particularly from those who have to compete for low-paid jobs with them. Usually takes decades to gain acceptance.

Step 3: Discussion [20m = 5m + 15m]

2.4   If your students have difficulty in generating ideas for the discussion, one way of stimulating them is to build up an ideas map gradually on the board by eliciting suggestions from them: start by writing 'World population explosion' on the board and asking 'Why is it a problem?, What are the consequences of the population explosion? What can be done to ease or solve the problem? An example of an ideas map built up from students' responses to these questions is shown on page 64.

SHEET C

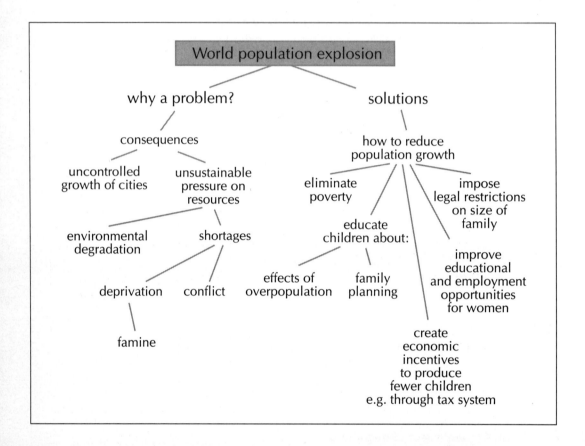

2.5 Tell the class how much time they will have for the discussion. Inform the class when half of this time has elapsed, and remind them that each individual should make sure he contributes at least two ideas before the end of the discussion.

 Step 4: Review [8m]

2.6 If you think it is more suitable for your class at this stage, use the more extensive **Reviewing Discussion: Checklist 3** on page 118 instead of the set of three review questions given here.

When students have had time in their pairs to discuss the questions, round up their ideas in a brief, whole-class discussion.

SESSION 3

If your students all come from the same country: In Task 3.1, ask students to speak not about their own country, but about different regions within their country. Or, alternatively, ask them to do a little library research in advance to enable them to talk about the situation in particular countries or regions of the world (e.g. Australia, Japan, Canada, Central Africa, Europe).

Step 1: Exchanging information [20m]

3.1 Divide the class into groups of three or four, ensuring as far as possible a mixture of backgrounds within each. Before instructing students to exchange information, quickly go through the questions with the class and deal with any queries that arise. You may need, for example, to clarify the meaning of *net immigration, emigration, braindrain* and *labour shortage*.

This task is more discursive than previous information-exchange tasks. It provides every individual student with confidence-building practice at discussing the topic of international migration. It also elicits from the group material that will be recycled and developed in subsequent tasks.

3.2 Provide students with blank OHTs or poster sheets, and pens, for them to produce visual aids. Each group should produce a display outline at least.

Step 2: Preparing to respond to questions [10m]

3.3 Possible answers:
1) Perhaps most likely to happen when questioner is at the front or on one side of a large audience, and when he asks the question unclearly, with the result that:
   • the presenter thinks that some of the audience may have been unable to hear or to understand what the questioner said
   • the presenter thinks that he may not have understood what the questioner said.
2) Clarifies the question for them and therefore makes the answer more meaningful.
3) Maintains rapport with audience as a whole.
   • Gives him some time to plan a response.
   • Reassures him that the answer he is planning is relevant to the question asked.

Step 3: Presentation [36m = 4 x (5m + 4m)]

3.4   As usual, ensure that presenters receive feedback on their presentations, from you and/or their peers. For written feedback, use either one of the checklists for **Assessing presentations** (pages 112-113) or a feedback note (see page xx for an example).

Step 4: Language review [10m]

See page xv for a note on this type of task.

UNIT 8

DEFENCE

SKILLS FOCUS: Generating ideas

You need to prepare: opinion cards (for Task 1.1); Extract A and Extract B on different cassette tapes and two tape recorders (or an arrangement with a colleague doing this activity at the same time) for the jigsaw listening in Task 2.1; OHTs or posters and pens for Task 3.4.

SESSION 1

Step 1: Language practice [20m]

1.1 **Preparation**

Before the session, prepare sets of six opinion cards appropriate for your class. For variety of interaction, ask the students to get into groups with people they have not worked with before. Give each group one set of cards and tell the students to take one card each, at random. There are more cards than students in each group, so that if a student really cannot speak on the topic selected there is an alternative.

The opinions on the cards need to be fairly controversial, so that speakers will be able to think of arguments quickly and listeners will have strong opposing views. Here are some suggestions:

- Allowing domestic pets (e.g. cats, dogs) into the house is unhygienic.
- The emotional development of young children is harmed if their mothers go out to work.
- Space exploration is a waste of the world's resources.
- Television does more harm than good.
- Working long hours has a dehumanising effect on people.
- Scientists are morally responsible for the effects of their discoveries.

Give students five minutes to think of (and note down) arguments and prepare in stage 3). Emphasise that they must speak for two minutes in support of the statement on the card, even if they do not agree with it. Point out that this is good practice in trying to anticipate other people's arguments or points of view, plus it is sometimes necessary to argue for a viewpoint you do not completely agree with.

1.2   **Giving a talk**

The two-minute time limit should be enforced here, including interruptions, as this is intended to be a warm-up activity.

At the end you could ask each group to nominate their most successful speaker and explain their choice.

Step 2: Generating ideas [10m]

1.3   1) Student suggestions here might include:

- national or regional defence
- collaboration with international forces (such as the United Nations)
- providing national emergency services (in cases of national or local disaster).

Step 3: Collecting questions [20m]

1.4   This is done individually. Other questions might include:

- Are there women in the British army?
- What is its role abroad?
- Who controls it?
- Who can join?
- What do British people feel about the army?
- Is it a volunteer or a conscripted army? (N.B. Try to ensure this question arises as this vocabulary will be needed later).

1.5   Write some of the students' questions on the board or OHP and together decide which six questions to keep for the next class. Ensure that at least one or two of the questions that come up in each extract (see 2.1 below) are in the class list.

1.6   Make sure the students copy down the six questions.

SESSION 2

This is a jigsaw listening task (see page xiv on conducting this type of task) with two extracts of approximately three minutes each from a recording of a British army officer, Captain Johnson, talking about the army in Britain today. The transcripts can be found on pages 97–99 in the Student's Book.

Step 1: Listening [15m]

2.1   Divide the class into two groups (A and B) to listen to the extracts, and make notes in answer to their list of questions and any other questions asked on the tape. You may wish to liaise with another teacher to do this activity, with all Extract A students from both classes in one room and Extract B in the other; this avoids having two tape recorders in your class. In either case, give control of the tape recorder to the students, or allow them to ask for the tape to be stopped on the second listening.

Tell the students to listen through once without stopping the tape, then to listen again, stopping when necessary to take notes. Set a limit of twelve minutes for 2.1.

The interview questions asked and notes of the main points made in the answers are as follows, with language that may need pre-teaching to the appropriate group underlined.

EXTRACT A

1.   **What is the role of the army in Britain today?**

    1. primarily as a defence force (in mainland Britain: training)

    2. Northern Ireland – a different role – to assist the <u>Royal Ulster Constabulary</u> (RUC) in the maintenance of law and order.

    N.B. The RUC is the Northern Irish police force.

2.   **What is the role of the British army, firstly, within NATO and, secondly, the UN?**

    1. within NATO – since Second World War – should any member state be invaded/under threat of invasion others would assist. That threat is now decreasing in the Western world – NATO is more of a political organisation to improve standards in all aspects of life, not just defence.

    2. UN – similar role; more recently: peacekeeping duties (e.g. keeping the Green Line in Cyprus since 1974). Also – early '90s – former Yugoslavia – assisting the UN in its peacekeeping role to keep the aid corridors open.

3.   **What challenges do you think there will be for the British army in the next century?**

    1. difficult to predict, because of the great changes in Europe

    2. keeping pace with changes in the world/keeping up with world events

    3. maintaining their defence role.

EXTRACT B

1. **Who joins the army?**
   1. applicants must be between $16\,^1/_2$ and 24; maximum age = 32, depending on qualifications
   2. minimum qualifications: 5 <u>GCSEs</u> (for officers); 3–5 GCSEs (for soldier trades depending on what they want to do)
   3. no <u>discrimination</u> against any sector of society – anyone can enter so long as they have the educational qualifications, are medically fit and pass the selection criteria.

   N.B. GCSEs are English secondary school qualifications (General Certificate of Secondary Education).

2. **What do you think are the advantages of having a <u>professional army</u> over a <u>conscripted army</u>?**
   1. people who enter want to join (<u>volunteers</u>)
   2. continuity – people are in for longer periods of time (minimum = 3 years, but average is 6–9 for soldiers and 6–8 for officers).

3. **Who controls the army?**

   Her Majesty the Queen is Commander in Chief of the army but control is passed to the government of the day, through the Ministry of Defence.

4. **How is the British army paid for?**

   By the Government – through the <u>Public Sector Budget</u> – so they take their share alongside Health, Social Security, Education.

   N.B. The Public Sector Budget is the amount of money allocated by the Government to pay for public services.

5. **How many people are in the army at the moment?**

   Approximately 150,000

Step 2: Checking [5m]

2.2   In their groups (A or B), students compare their answers to the questions and discuss their notes.

Step 3: Second listening [10m]

2.3   Students listen again (with pausing/repetition) to confirm their information.

Step 4: Exchanging information [20m]

2.4   Pair each student with another who listened to the other extract. Students exchange information and complete their answers to the class questions from 1.6 as far as possible.

2.5   Students exchange any other information they have from the extracts.

Step 5: Before the next session

2.6   Emphasise to students that this is a crucial part of the next session and the points they wish to make must be carefully prepared and rehearsed.

SESSION 3

Step 1: Discussion [30m]

3.1   Allow each group to decide how they will conduct this discussion. Point out that everyone must have a chance to speak and that there is a time limit of 30 minutes. They should begin by deciding on their procedure, which could be one of the following:

- a series of short talks: each person in turn speaking for five minutes, with some questions at the end of each talk.
- a discussion: one person gives their talk until another person wants to interrupt and take over the discussion with a point of similarity/difference with regard to the army in their country/a different perspective. Other students to join in when they want to.
- the group decides on one or two key questions from the prompt questions on page 115 of the Student's Book and they then discuss those.

Step 2: Review [10m]

3.2   Encourage students to think about and analyse what made any particular explanation successful. This will depend on what format the discussion took in 3.1, but answers could include:

- a speaker with clear, consistent ideas
- a speaker with a limited number of points to make
- a speaker who puts his ideas simply
- a speaker who gives memorable examples
- a speaker who realises when his listeners have not understood and who then rephrases his point.

3.3   Encourage students to think carefully about their own contribution to the discussion and the improvements they will try to make next time.

Step 3: Discussion and reporting back [50m]

3.4   Give students five minutes to think individually about the topic and note down their thoughts. Put them into groups of up to five people to discuss the topic, asking each group to appoint a secretary to take notes of the main ideas.

Emphasise the need for clear notes on the OHT or poster, as there is not enough time to rewrite them. Each group must also identify who will speak in 3.5.

Timing: They must be ready to report back to the class after 25 minutes and each group will have five minutes for their report.

Ideas that could be suggested include:

- by joining together with other countries to form defence groups
- by financial and economic strength
- by the threat of total warfare and annihilation
- through an international peacekeeping organisation
- with national armies
- by spying and attacking from satellites in space
- by controlling global communications
- by scientific knowledge.

3.5   Groups then report their views back to the rest of the class, with five minutes each. Four groups is probably the maximum here, so you will need to select groups if the class if larger than this.

 ## Step 4: Language review [10m]

See page xv for a note on conducting this type of task.

UNIT 9

PARAPSYCHOLOGY

SKILLS FOCUS: Rehearsing and evaluating

SESSION 1

Step 1: Warm-up [10m]

1.1 This task orients students to the topic and the basic questions dealt with in the unit. The intention is not to discuss them exhaustively at this stage – similar questions will be discussed at greater length later in the unit (Session 3, Step 4).

Notice that students will not be able to discuss questions 2 to 4 properly until they are clear about question 1. So, establish the answer to question 1 with the whole class first, and then put students into small groups of three or four to quiz each other about questions 2 to 4.

If a convenient opportunity arises at the reporting-back stage, establish the meaning of some of the vocabulary that might otherwise be problematic in the reading text for the next two tasks (e.g. *crank, fraud, isolated, steel-lined cubicle*).

Step 2: Reading and prediction [20m = 5m + 15m]

The text used as source material in this unit is longer and denser than texts used in earlier units, and the jigsaw task (1.4 and following) is more demanding. Tasks 1.2 and 1.3 are intended to make the jigsaw reading (1.4) more manageable by leading students into the text gradually.

1.2 Put students into pairs for this task. Emphasise that the focus here is on predicting the content of the text as a whole, not on picking up new vocabulary. If this kind of prediction task is new to your students, you may need to prompt them along the following lines: 'The title of the text clearly suggests that the text is about telepathy, but in what connection? What issues or questions related to telepathy do you think it will consider? What do you think later paragraphs/sections in the text will be about? …'

Allow two or three minutes for students to arrive at a prediction, then ask some of the pairs to tell the class what their prediction is. Draw out any unclear or particularly interesting points.

1.3 For most classes this is probably best done in two stages – pairs or small groups, then whole class. Make sure at the whole-class stage that all students have grasped the gist of these opening paragraphs, otherwise the homework and subsequent tasks will be unnecessarily troublesome.

KEY

1) Part of an experiment to test whether people can transmit images telepathically.

2) They regard it as being largely unproductive and often flawed.

Step 3: Before the next session

1.4 Direct one third of your students to Text A on pages 64-65, another third to Text B on pages 76-77, and the final third to Text C on pages 80-81. Each student is to look at **one** text only. Check that they understand the task outlined in the Student's Book. Some of the less common words in the text are glossed in footnotes, but students will probably want to use their dictionaries. Make it clear that, although the homework task requires them to understand the gist of their text, they do not need to understand every single word.

Session 2

The overall purpose of the tasks in this session is to prepare students for the jigsaw presentation task in Session 3 by reaching a common understanding within their group as to the content of their text, and then planning and rehearsing their presentation.

Step 1: Language focus [5m]

2.1 See page xiv for a note on this type of task.

Step 2: Discussion [5m]

2.2 Circulate, monitoring each group in turn, to check that its discussion is moving along the right lines; intervene where necessary, to help the group recognise what the main points of its text are.

2.3 Be ready to provide concise answers to students' questions about the texts.

Step 3: Rehearsal and evaluation [20m]

2.4 The value of rehearsal for the EAP learner is stressed in the Introduction (page x of the Students' Book), where *'Think, plan and rehearse for tasks'* is one of the six tips for getting the most out of the course, and in the model for **Preparing a**

presentation, in which Step 8 is 'Rehearse and evaluate' (page 114 of the Students' Book). You may want to refer students to one of these briefly, before proceeding with the task.

Each pair should go through the following sequence:

1) Student A says which aspect(s) of his summary he wants feedback on.

2) Student A presents his summary.

3) Student B gives feedback.

4) Student B says which aspect(s) of his summary he wants feedback on.

5) Student B presents his summary.

6) Student A gives feedback.

Help students with the timing here, by telling them, when seven or eight minutes have elapsed, that it is time for Student B to give feedback and then start his own summary.

Round this off with a whole-class stage, in which you ask three or four individual students to say what they have learned from the rehearsal and feedback, and how they think it may enable them to improve their summary next time. If you have a relatively weak class, you may want your students to write down two improvements that they intend to make to their summary as a result of the rehearsal and feedback.

Step 4: Before the next session [15m]

SESSION 3

Step 1: Presenting [20m]

3.1   Remind the class that each student has a maximum of five minutes to present his summary. If necessary, help students with the timing by chivvying them after five minutes ('The first presenter should be finishing now. The other group members have two minutes to ask questions about unclear content, then it will be the second presenter's turn.') and again after twelve minutes.

Step 2: At the end of each talk [5m]

3.2   This questioning should be done within the group; the questions should be addressed to the speaker concerned. Monitor, and clear up any important misunderstandings or uncertainties about content which students cannot resolve themselves.

Step 3: At the end of all three talks [10m]

3.3
and
3.4
Allow time for students to carry out this exchange of views within their group at first. Then spend a few minutes in a whole-class session asking a few students to report on the most interesting points that emerged in their group.

Step 4: Discussion [35m]

3.5
Allow three or four minutes for students individually to note down their answers to the questions.

3.6
Before groups start organising the case for or against, raise with them the importance (especially in an academic context) of citing evidence in support of their argument. Establish how long the spokespeople are going to have (in Task 3.7) to put forward their group's views. You can give the group the option of dividing its points up between two or more speakers.

3.7
Tell students to listen carefully to the arguments put forward and to judge which they find more persuasive. Restrict the time taken up by the main speakers, to ensure that there is enough time left at the end for you to open up discussion to the class as a whole. Finally, ask students for a quick show of hands to indicate whether they believe psychic abilities exist or not.

Step 5: Language review [12m]

See page xv for a note on this type of task.

UNIT
10

STUDYING IN A NEW ENVIRONMENT

SKILLS FOCUS: Summarising in discussion

You need to prepare: cassette(s) and cassette player(s) for Task 2.1; blank OHTs or poster sheets, and pens, for Task 2.7.

Note: the timing of the sessions in this unit is different from that in previous units. So that we could devote the final session of this final unit exclusively to review and round-up activities, we have placed the extended listening activity in Session 2. As a result, Session 2 is the long session in this unit, instead of Session 3.

Session 1

Step 1: Warm-up [8m]

1.1   This is probably best done in three stages:

1) two minutes for students individually to note down their ideas

2) three minutes for students in groups of three or four to share their ideas

3) three minutes for a whole-class round-up of the most interesting points.

Step 2: Reading [10m]

1.2   One way of leading into this task is to ask the class whether any of them have ever experienced 'culture shock'. If they are uncertain of the meaning of this expression, you can ask them to guess it from the constituent words.

Step 3: Language focus [10m]

1.3   See page xiv for a note on this type of task.

1.4   Allow time for students in pairs or groups to discuss various possible sequences, before you tell them what in fact the original sequence was.

KEY

Stage no.	Description of stage
4	*You thought you had got used to it, but one or two minor things go wrong and it feels as if the whole world is against you. Some people give up at this stage, or become aggressive or withdrawn.*
1	*Excitement.*
5	*Adjustment to the new environment takes place. You either integrate into the new culture, or decide that you don't like it but have to tolerate it temporarily.*
3	*You begin to get used to it.*
2	*Culture shock. A few things start to go wrong. Differences between your own culture and the new culture start to cause problems. What was once new and exciting now seems unfamiliar and frustrating.*

Step 4: Discussion [10m]

1.5 In groups of four. Monitor the discussion. If group members do not feel (in their discussion of questions 1 and 2 that Woolfenden's five stages correspond to their own experience at all, ask them to try to outline an alternative series of stages that do reflect their own experience.

As for question 3, the 'difficult stages' are presumably stage 2 and stage 4. This question anticipates the content of Session 2, where students listen to advice from people who have just completed their courses.

SESSION 2

Step 1: Listening [25m]

2.1 See page xv for a note on procedures to use with this type of jigsaw listening task. Prepare students for the listening task by directing them to the rubric in the Student's Book and eliciting some possible examples of 'the challenges that face international students'. If the opportunity arises here, pre-teach language items that you think might otherwise present problems for your students in the listening texts (tapescripts on pages 100–105 of Student's Book).

The texts are adapted from interviews with Li, a Chinese MA student of Applied Linguistics, and Chris, a British MSc student of Agricultural Extension and Rural Development. If you have anyone in your class who is particularly interested in either of these fields, you can steer him towards the appropriate listening text.

2.2 Monitor students' notes and discussions here, to ensure that they are on the right lines, otherwise the value of Step 2 is much diminished.

ADVICE FOR INTERNATIONAL STUDENTS FROM SPEAKER 1(LI)

Cultural differences

Accept that these will exist.

Be tolerant of them, so that you can work with other students.

Expect similar acceptance and tolerance from them.

Study groups

Select students who live near you and who have a similar approach to study.

Be flexible in co-operating with them.

Tutor

Establish what kind of support you are entitled to (try reading the departmental handbook).

But remember that tutors vary: work out the most effective approach with your particular tutor.

Prepare for meetings so as to avoid wasting time: list points in advance in your order of priority.

Facilities on campus

Explore campus early on, to locate facilities (e.g. libraries, advisory services, Students' Union).

In library, familiarise yourself with sections likely to be relevant to your studies. Enquire about specialist collections.

Make use of advisory services, e.g. consult Applied Statistics advisory service early on about the design of an experimental project.

Make use of the Students' Union – it is run *by* students *for* students. You can contact the Overseas Students' Committee, who have experience of your situation and want to improve it. The Union is also valuable as an information centre (about items for sale, accommodation to share, activities to take part in). The club activities (e.g. chess, mountaineering) are a good way to unwind, and to socialise with a wide range of students, both home and international.

Style of lecture

Be prepared for a lecture style in which contributions from the audience are often invited.

Practise so that you can join in. Do not discuss privately during lectures.

Approaching your course

See the course as a whole from the start: what is the most important part of it in terms of assessment and learning? If there is a dissertation, jot down ideas for it from early on in the course.

ADVICE FOR INTERNATIONAL STUDENTS FROM SPEAKER 2 (CHRIS)

Tutors

Make full use of them.

Find out early on at what times they will be available for tutorial appointments.

Don't be shy about approaching them with questions. If you have a serious problem, report it to your tutor immediately.

If you don't have a personal tutor, take questions and problems to the lecturer instead.

Reading

Be selective.

Ask tutor to prioritise if necessary.

Study resources

At the library, make use of the recall system.

Talk your assignments over with fellow students: your initial ideas, your progress, difficulties you experience.

Try forming a study group, to work for an assignment or an exam. Select people who live conveniently nearby and with whom you can work easily. Studying in this way can be more enjoyable and more efficient (the workload is shared, and problems are clarified through discussion), and it gives you practice in expressing yourself.

Choosing options

Choose according to subject, not according to who is offering the option. An option in which you are genuinely interested is a better source of motivating topics for a dissertation.

Dissertation or long essay

Draft a proposal and seek a meeting early on to discuss it with your tutor.

Draw up a work schedule, with a reasonable deadline for each successive stage of the project. This is good for morale, as it makes the project seem manageable and gives you a sense of progress.

Step 2: Summarising in discussion [25m]

2.3 Give students two or three minutes individually to note down their answers to these questions. Then quickly go through them, eliciting, to establish the form and function of this kind of summarising. If the opportunity arises as you elicit, demonstrate by summarising what one of the students has just said to you.

Notes on the questions:

1. If so, in what circumstances?

2. Probably when one speaker had made a fairly lengthy point and the other person is not sure he has fully understood it.

3. No doubt the purpose differs from one occasion to another, but amongst the objects it may achieve are the following:

- The speaker finds out whether he understood the previous speaker's point.
- The previous speaker then has the opportunity to rectify any misunderstanding.
- It may refocus the discussion after a long, rambling contribution from the previous speaker.

4. 'So, ...' seems to be the word most frequently used to introduce a summary of this kind, in a wide range of contexts. Refer students to the Language Help section for possible responses.

2.4 Encourage your students to make at least one or two attempts at summarising the point just made by their interlocutor. The processing load involved makes this a demanding task – students have simultaneously to comprehend what their interlocutor is saying and to compose a summary of it.

Monitor to offer help and feedback. When all students have completed the task, briefly review it with them:

Did they all make one or two attempts at summarising?

How effectively did they manage to do it?

Did they find that it served the purpose referred to above (Task 2.3, question 3)?

What difficulties did they find?

2.5 Circulate to give the pairs some feedback on their ideas here.

Step 3: Group task [15m]

2.6 Put students in groups of four or five. Tell them that they can produce the advice sheet in note form, using bullet points, etc., as appropriate; it does not need to be a polished piece of writing.

If you want to provide your students with additional input for this task, the book by Jane Woolfenden, which is cited in the Students' Book, is a good source. It has sections headed, for example, 'Getting used to a new life', 'Things you may find disappointing', 'Surviving disappointment', 'Feeling at home in Britain', 'Dos and don'ts in case of depression', 'Hospitality schemes', 'Female students and wives of students', 'The Student Union', 'Social life and entertainment', and 'If you get lonely'. It contains, for instance, a list of practical suggestions as to what someone can do in order to feel at home in a new environment: students could be asked to evaluate the suggestions, or to find out from their partner which of them he has already carried out.

Example of work produced by students for Task 2.6

ADVICE SHEET FOR NEW STUDENTS

1. Places where you can meet other people:
   - Union coffee bar
   - International Students' Club
   - your departmental common room
2. Some practical information
   - getting your photocopying done cheaply
   - opening a bank account
   - paying bills (phone, electricity, etc.)
   - registering with the police
   - finding accommodation
3. People you can consult when you have a problem
   - tutor
   - warden in hall of residence
   - student welfare officer
   - counselling service
4. Weather tip
   - Carry an umbrella with you at all times!

2.7   Here, and in the following task, students prepare and use brief headings on an OHT or poster as the basis of a short presentation. It is an opportunity for you to ask the weaker students, who may have found this difficult earlier in the course, to discover how much they have improved.

Step 4: Reporting back [25m]

2.8   Produce some form of written feedback for each presenter, using either one of the checklists for **Assessing presentations** (pages 112-113) or a feedback note (page xix).

Session 3

Step 1: Assessing your progress [20m]

3.1   Remind students of the self-assessment that they carried out at the beginning of the course, but tell them *not* to look back at that page for the time being. The purpose of this task is to help students assess the progress that they have made over the course.

3.2 When students have had time in their pairs to discuss these questions, ask some of them to report back to the whole class. The original self-assessment table is on page 109 of the Students' Book.

Step 2: Looking to the future [25m]

3.3 One of the questions in this exercise asks students 'What will you do after this course to make further progress?' This may lead to questions about other courses/services provided by your institution. For example, if you are using this book as part of a pre-sessional course, be ready to explain to students what continuing English language support is available to students during their departmental course.

3.4 To enable students to take away a useful record of the ideas that come up in this session, gradually build up on the board a list or ideas map of the points that emerge from 3.4 and 3.5; suggest that students should make a similar map of their own.

3.5 Do your best to provide some suggestions relevant to the particular circumstances of your students.

One of the most important steps for students to take after the course, in order to go on improving their spoken English, is to socialise in English as often as possible. As well as mixing with colleagues in their own department (as advocated strongly by John Mitchell in the Foundation Unit), and with other students in the college/university at large (as recommended by Li in Session 2 of Unit 10, when she talks about joining university clubs and societies), international students in an English-speaking country would also benefit from any social contacts they can make outside the college/university.

Some colleges/universities in the UK organise programmes of events to bring their international students into contact socially with people and families in the local community. There is also a national, non-profit-making organisation which arranges for international students at British universities to spend some time (for example, a bank holiday weekend, or the Christmas period) with a British family: The Host Organisation, 18 Northumberland Avenue, London WC2N 5AP.